W

To the second edition of the Ultimate Guide to Cloud Computing - an in-depth look at all things cloud.

CLOUD IS SUCH A BROAD TOPIC worthy of an entire guide for each sub strand and service available. However, we realise time is a precious commodity so we've tried to distill the essentials into this Ultimate Guide.

If you're new to the concept, this guide will arm you with the knowledge you need to understand more about how cloud computing fits into your life – as both a consumer or a business user.

Conversely, if you're already familiar with cloud computing, this guide will serve as a decision making aid in working out what your next steps should be with greater confidence.

In addition to background information about what cloud computing is and what it can do for you, we also detail the different types of cloud and provide a reality check as to the pros and cons of moving your tech skywards.

There are also case studies describing the journeys of those who've been there and done that as well as the nitty gritty on money, contract issues and more.

Once you've made your cloud-focused decisions, it's time to choose a partner. You'll be pleased to hear we've got service provider selection covered, too, in addition to an A-Z listing of the key partners out there.

Importantly, we're not here to push you in one direction or the other when it comes to cloud. Yes, it's the way the industry is moving and there will come a point in time when those who haven't at the very least tried to understand what cloud is will be at a disadvantage. But you need to move at a pace and level you're comfortable with.

With that in mind, this guide will advise and detail rather than dictate or demand. We hope you find it insightful and informative.

Thanks for reading.

Maggie Holland, Editor

EDITORIAL
Editor Maggie Holland
Consulting editor Maxwell Cooter
Design & Layout Heather Reeves
Contributors Marc Beishon, Simon Brew, Adrian Bridgwater, Dave Cartwright, Graham Jarvis, Frank Jennings, Billy MacInnes, Lesley Meall, Rene Millman, Mark Samuels, Davey Winder

LICENSING & SYNDICATION
Licensing Carlotta Serantoni, carlotta_serantoni@dennis.co.uk, +44 20 7907 6550
Syndication Anj Dosaj-Halai, Anj_Dosaj-Halai@dennis.co.uk, +44 20 7907 6132

ADVERTISING & MARKETING
Advertising Manager
Ben Topp +44 20 7907 6625
MagBook Account Manager
Katie Wood +44 20 7907 6689
Digital Production Manager
Nicky Baker +44 20 7907 6056
Marketing & Editorial Executive
Paul Goodhead +44 20 7907 6393

MANAGEMENT +44 20 7907 6000
MagBook Publisher Dharmesh Mistry
Publishing Director Jon Westnedge
Managing Director John Garewal
Deputy Managing Director Tim Danton
MD of Advertising Julian Lloyd-Evans
Newstrade Director David Barker
Chief Operating Officer Brett Reynolds
Group Finance Director Ian Leggett
Chief Executive James Tye
Chairman Felix Dennis

MAGBOOK 

Printed by Stones

The Ultimate Guide To Cloud Computing
ISBN 1781060924

INSIDE

04 What is cloud?
What is cloud computing and how can it benefit you?

08 Cloud types
What do the different cloud types mean and which is right for you?

12 Cloud benefits
The top reasons for moving to the cloud.

20

24

14 Cloud concerns
What puts people off cloud?

20 The future
Where next for cloud?

24 Business agility
How will the cloud impact your business?

28 Cloud and the board
How can executives prepare?

36 Cloud and SMEs
What's in it for small businesses?

WIN A KINDLE
See page 19

41 Cloud contracts
Pay heed to the T&Cs when it comes to cloud contracts.

48 Cloud storage
Where and how data is stored matters.

52 Cloud security
Keeping data safe is key in the cloud.

56 Finance and budgeting
Do the cost benefits add up?

62 Environment
Is the cloud as green as we think?

66 Cloud case studies
Those with cloud history talk about their experiences.

80 Choosing a provider
Advice on choosing the right partner for your cloud project.

86 Cloud provider A to Z
A who's who of the cloud world.

94 Glossary
Key cloud terms demystified and explained.

What is cloud?

What is cloud computing and where did it come from? More importantly, how can it help you?

EVERYBODY IS TALKING about cloud computing. But what does it actually mean? It's certainly not the easiest of terms to define and there have been many different attempts to explain what it all actually means. Thus far, some cloud companies have been prone, much like Alice's Humpty Dumpty, to define the term in a way that they want it to mean. All very convenient.

In some ways it's strange that the term has been so slippery. Millions of us are happy to use such cloud-based services as Facebook, Gmail and Twitter, thinking nothing of it, yet pinning down an exact definition has been as elusive as grabbing a cloud itself.

In an attempt to put a stop to these vagaries, the US National Institute of Standards and Technology put forward a definition that has now become widely accepted as the closest that the industry has to a definitive answer. The NIST definition is as follows.

"Cloud computing is a model for enabling, convenient, on-demand network access to a shared pool of configurable computing resources (e.g. networks, servers, storage, applications, and services) that can be rapidly provisioned and released with minimal management effort or service provider interaction. This cloud model promotes availability and is composed of five essential characteristics, three service models, and four deployment models."

The service models are types of

offering, such as Software-as-a-Service (SaaS), and deployment choices include public and private clouds. But the key characteristics of cloud from a customer's point of view are:

- Self-provisioning, so a customer can provision facilities without any human interaction;
- Delivery of services over a network;
- Ability to be accessed by a variety of devices, not just PCs but also by netbooks, tablet computers and smartphones;
- Rapid 'elasticity' – the ability to scale up or scale down computing resources. From a cloud provider's point of view, a major element of the process is the pooling of computing resources to serve multiple consumers, using what's called a multi-tenant model whereby cloud services are provided to customers as and when they're needed. One of the important factors for cloud service providers is to be able to measure usage accurately and, even more importantly, to bill accurately.

Security concerns

The factor in cloud services that makes most users nervous is the level of security within a multi-tenant model. This is a major concern. Customers are entrusting some of their sensitive data to a third party and there is, of course, nothing stopping one of their major competitors going to the same cloud provider for a service.

Service providers believe that this concern can be easily dealt with: they've generally had a long history of keeping customers' data safe and have levels of security that far exceed those of their customers. Take Amazon, one of the leading lights in cloud technology. Millions of us around the world are willing to entrust our personal details and credit cards to that company believing they'll be held safely – why should trusting the company's cloud division, Amazon Web Services, be any different?

In many ways, a more important consideration than security is the location of the data. This is for two reasons. First, there is the inherent latency within the system: the further away the data is stored the longer the lag in accessing it. This is becoming less of a problem as network connections get faster but it still can be a factor.

The second problem is a more serious one, particularly on this side of the Atlantic. There are various EU regulations on where data can be stored – personal data cannot be held outside the EU (within the EU itself, individual countries

Difference between outsourcing and cloud computing

Outsourcing is widely known and used in technology circles. It's when a third party performs an IT function or other service on behalf of its customer. Outsourcing can be employed for a variety of reasons – lack of expertise in-house, lack of personnel or because the resources are needed purely for an individual project.

The key differences with cloud are defined by the underlying technology of the cloud provider. Essential to this is the use of virtualisation – all cloud providers make use of virtualisation technology – and automation (the ideal cloud service has little human intervention). The other key element of cloud computing is the use of self-provisioning – one of the major benefits is the ability to make a business more agile and flexible because services can be turned up and down at will.

"According to an oft-cited Gartner report, 20 per cent of enterprises will have no IT departments by the end of 2012."

have stricter guidelines still). This has been a problem for some cloud providers, as part of the appeal is that unused resources at one data centre can be used by another. If data centres outside the EU cannot store European customers' data, providers have to be careful in marshalling their resources.

Allied to this is a secondary problem: the US Patriot Act, which compels US companies to hand over personal data held on their servers if requested by US authorities. As this applies to European data held on servers located in Europe, this has made some European customers rather nervous. The implications of the Patriot Act are still being worked through.

Virtual world

There are other elements within cloud computing. Virtualisation is another key concept involving the use of virtual resources instead of physical ones. For example, a server within a data centre may be operating at just 15 per cent of its capacity (this used to be a typical usage); virtualisation is a technique where the resources that aren't being used by the server for the application that it's driving (database, website or whatever) can be used for something else – driving usage rates up. Virtualisation will often go hand-in-hand with server consolidation so it helps to reduce the number of servers within a data centre.

Cloud computing: A brief history

Anyone hanging around cloud vendors for any amount of time will hear one often repeated mantra – "Cloud computing is not new you know, cloud has been around for some time" – generally from a veteran of the technology industry. There's an element of truth in this but, at the same time, it's spectacularly missing the point.

It's possible to point to a 1966 book by Douglas Parkhill, *The Challenge of the Computer Utility*, for the origins of cloud computing. In that book, Parkhill detailed many of the elements of cloud computing – elastic provision, online delivery, perception of infinite supply – it's just taken a while for the theory to become reality.

Saying that the theories espoused in Parkhill's book are the first elements of cloud computing is a bit like saying that Leonardo Da Vinci's notebooks are the blueprints for the first helicopter. It's one thing coming forward with the theory, it's quite another delivering in practice. There have been plenty of false dawns before cloud computing became the beast it has become. We've seen it described as grid computing, computing on-demand and utility computing before the phrase cloud computing took hold. It's only been widely used since late 2007, although the term was first used in a lecture by computer scientist Ramnath Chellappa.

For cloud computing to become a reality, there were other changes needed first. Most important of these was the availability of fast and cheap broadband – the early attempts at cloud computing all foundered because of the dearth of such a service. Then virtualisation needed to become more widespread, as this technology is the bedrock of cloud computing.

Other factors are the declining cost in storage, the availability of cheaper devices to access cloud services and the development of automatic provisioning software.

Like cloud computing, it's an old concept, originating from the mainframe world and only becoming widely used after VMware, a virtualisation specialist, started applying it to servers. The technology has now been adopted nearly universally within enterprises and the technique of re-allocating resources has made it vital for the development of the cloud.

We've spoken a lot about cloud service providers but another important part of the cloud is the delivery of software – the so-called SaaS delivery mechanism. This is a technique that was really pioneered by Salesforce.com with its hosted CRM product, but has since been adopted by countless other companies. SaaS delivery helps solve various problems within an enterprise: over-provisioning, security updates and licensing among them, and is widely seen now as the dominant method for providing software.

As a concept, cloud computing has grown quickly and is set to penetrate deeper into the market. According to an oft-cited Gartner report, 20 per cent of enterprises will have no IT departments by the end of 2012. While that looks to be a bit optimistic (or pessimistic depending on your view), the impetus is clearly with cloud. It's a technology that's here to stay. ■

PUBLIC OR PRIVATE: Which way should you go?

It's not just about whether to move and when, once you've decided that, then comes the question of public, private or hybrid

MUCH OF THE DEBATE about cloud computing has focused on two distinct types of operation: Public and private. While they are often bundled under the convenient term of cloud computing, they are very different operational beasts.

Public started with Amazon

Public cloud, which is simply using the web to access computer services of one sort or another can be linked back to Amazon's 2002 move to leverage its vast infrastructure to offer computer facilities to customers. The company launched a range of services to developers, including storage and a development platform.

Amazon's initiative, which preceded the phrase 'cloud computing' itself, has been followed by the likes of Apple, Google et al and a selection of hosting companies as they seek to capture the interest in this approach.

This is somewhat of a throwback to the concept of the computer bureau, where companies paid a monthly fee to buy mainframe time. It's a business that seemed to die a death when PCs and the client-server model came into play.

Like the computer bureau, public cloud providers charge their customers on a monthly basis – generally according to gigabytes transmitted and bandwidth used. The crucial aspect being that the cloud provider bears the entire cost of running the infrastructure. This means customers don't have to worry about maintenance or staffing help desks. Nor do they have to worry about investing in storage hardware, a growing budgetary strain on organisations as data storage volumes move ever upwards.

Crucially, it also frees organisations from capacity planning concerns. This can be a big headache for companies with seasonal fluctuations, where they might have over-provisioned for peak traffic. That's a big pain that the new breed of cloud providers can deal with instead.

So, public cloud offers a number of advantages to organisations, particularly small businesses and start-ups, both of whom generally lack large enough tech teams and may be reluctant to tie up capital on IT infrastructure.

There are, however, downsides too. The main disadvantage with public cloud is that there can be some security issues. Companies will have to hand over confidential data to a third party and for many firms this is a move too far. There will be worries about customer data being released into the public domain, concerns about companies being

> **"There are some commentators who claim that the idea of a private cloud is an oxymoron and that we should be talking about data centres instead."**

held legally responsible for breaches of privacy legislation and worries about sensitive data being held on a server, particularly where two competitors might be hosted.

But, especially if you're starting small, public cloud will almost certainly be the way to go. It is capable of handling something as small as a basic client contact database for a couple of salespeople as well as catering to other needs too.

What's more, many providers also offer simple storage services for single users.

In control with private cloud

The genesis of the private cloud was very different. There's no public operator and everything – hardware and software – is provided by you, the user. It sounds little different from a more conventional data centre, where your servers and applications are hosted by a specialist provider. Indeed there are some commentators who claim that the idea of a private cloud is an oxymoron, and that we should really be talking about data centres instead.

Proponents of private clouds maintain there is a difference. The main features ▶

"This is somewhat of a throwback to the concept of the computer bureau, where companies paid a monthly fee to buy mainframe time."

of a private cloud are a 'virtualised' infrastructure coupled with software that allows IT users to treat it as a centralised pool of computing resources.

Other features include automation, meaning that many of these tasks are handled without the intervention of an IT department. In turn, this removes the ability to measure and monitor what resources have been allocated to different departments, which could result in companies being unable to introduce chargeback for resources that have been consumed.

In the private cloud set-up, you have responsibility for buying the hardware and software, maintaining it and managing storage. As such, private cloud doesn't offer so many advantages when it comes to managing cash flow.

But there are other advantages. You connect to public cloud providers by using web connections, which can be very slow. This means that anyone trying to shift large files around would find the experience a lot of slower. On the other hand, private cloud infrastructures often use private connections, offering a much speedier experience, although there are issues for branch offices that may need to use a slower wide area network to get access to the main corporate link.

In addition, the private cloud doesn't have the security issues that could cause problems for public cloud users. All data is retained by your company and you control all access through a private firewall.

What's important here is that not only do you keep tabs on data, you also know exactly where, geographically speaking, it's being held. This not an academic principle, as there are important legal restraints on where data can or cannot be held and companies have to be wary of their statutory duty for protecting customer information.

Why not go hybrid?

There's no need to choose between private or public, as organisations with more than basic needs for cloud IT can opt for both in a hybrid approach, with some services in a private cloud, others in a public one. This could still be managed by one provider and can address concerns like holding sensitive data – such as customer credit card details – only on a private basis.

In an interview with Cloud Pro's sister title IT Pro at the end of 2011,

PUBLIC VS PRIVATE CLOUD: pros and cons

PUBLIC PROS
- Less expensive than private clouds
- More accessible than private clouds
- Short-term or temporary commitments
- Faster to deploy a single user than private clouds

PRIVATE PROS
- Can be secured to meet compliance at almost every level
- Single tenant environments eliminate the possibility of other companies affecting performance
- Private data centres usually accessible to IT auditors
- Customisable to meet an individual organisation's needs, rather than the mass approach of public clouds

PUBLIC CONS
- Fewer user management controls
- One-size-fits all approach (not tailored to a single organisation's or user's needs)
- Impersonal support, often via email, chat, or FAQs only
- Security and uptime might not meet enterprise compliance standards

PRIVATE CONS
- More expensive to deploy and maintain than public clouds
- May have longer-term commitments than public clouds
- May have less flexibility since hardware is dedicated to a single organisation

SOURCE: WWW.FOGODATACENTERS.COM

Bilhar Mann, vice president of CA Technologies' cloud business unit, suggested the future would be dominated by hybrid deployments.

"We believe the enterprise is going to be a hybrid environment. There's going to be some things in the public cloud, some things in the private cloud and some things will run the way they've run before," he said.

"Financial services companies amplify the complete spectrum of things. They've got mainframe technologies and at the other extreme they have web-based iPhone apps. They will have that complete spectrum of [cloud] technologies too."

CA Technologies is not alone in its viewpoint. Indeed, analysts see the value of the hybrid model too.

"Hybrid IT is the new IT and it is here to stay," said Chris Howard, managing vice president of analyst firm Gartner in May 2012.

"While the cloud market matures, IT organisations must adopt a hybrid IT strategy that not only builds internal clouds to house critical IT services and compete with public CSPs [cloud service providers], but also utilises the external cloud to house non-critical IT."

He added: "Hybrid IT creates symmetry between internal and external IT services that will force an IT and business paradigm shift for years to come."

Ultimately, the choice of which way to go will be based on a number of concerns unique to your business and the type of industry you operate in. ■

Benefiting from the cloud

The cloud has something to offer everyone - whether consumer or business, large or small

WE'VE ALREADY LOOKED at what the cloud is and explained the differences between public, private and hybrid but if you still need convincing of the merits of this model, read on for a run down of the top 10 benefits.

1 Cost savings

One of the biggest arguments for moving to the cloud is the cost savings on offer. Renting a car and paying for it only when you need it is cheaper than owning one and having to pay all the up front associated costs like tax and insurance. This financial element is mirrored in the cloud where paying as you go is more cost effective and attractive than a full-blown ownership model.

2 Better budgeting

Moving from cap ex to op ex is cited as one of the other major cost advantages of cloud computing. It tends to make accounting and budgeting much easier as you're not buying hardware and software yourself - you're simply renting infrastructure and services from a cloud provider who has made such investments.

3 Flexibility and stability

Workers can collaborate on the same projects across time zones and office boundaries and if new tools are needed they can quickly and easily be added to the existing environment. What's more, you can be sure you're using the most up to date version of any software you're running from those in the cloud - something you wouldn't necessarily get if you paid under the old licensing model.

4 Security

Far from making data less secure, many argue the cloud is actually more secure than the physical world. Cloud providers go to great lengths to ensure only authorised users have access to your data and invest big bucks to try to stay one step ahead of the bad guys. They're also subject to strict compliance criteria and certification around security, meaning it's part of their job to safeguard you and your data.

5 Scalability

The ability to scale up your infrastructure, platforms and software and shrink down again to the way you were before means firms can better respond to peaks and troughs in demand. Historically, companies would have had to purchase kit and software based on predicted demand. And pay for it up front too, crossing their fingers and hoping they had got it right. Cloud computing removes all this guess work.

6 Performance

It's often said there are no guarantees in life. The cloud world is different. Cloud service providers pride themselves on their service level agreements and performance pedigree. They're so confident in their claims they'll often promise financial compensation should systems go down.

7 Agility

Speed to market is a big deal when it comes to competitive advantage. Trying to build certain applications in-house versus opting for a hosted model just doesn't make commercial sense sometimes. Why reinvent the wheel unnecessarily? What's more, by partnering with established cloud providers you can more proactively respond to market changes and customer demand, rather than simply being reactive.

8 Productivity

The dream of anywhere, anytime access to data is finally a reality thanks to the cloud. Staff can be productive wherever they are, making them better able to service customers and maintain a better work/life balance. The happier the employee, the healthier the business' bottom line becomes, generally speaking. Of course, consumers can also make the most of any previous 'dead' time by having their documents and applications a mere click away, wherever they are.

9 The green factor

Opinions are mixed as to just how green the cloud can be. However, there's no doubting having less physical equipment on your premises will lessen your individual carbon footprint as well as being much more energy efficient. What's the point of having powered-up servers in the corner of a room just in case? None. This is something both your bank manager and Mother Nature agree on.

10 Focus

By trusting your applications, services or infrastructure to a cloud service provider, you can free up valuable tech time to focus on your core business and add value elsewhere. By partnering with the experts in cloud, you're free to continue to be an expert in your chosen field.

Are you scared of the big, bad cloud?

Cloud computing offers many benefits, but like any technology concept it's not entirely concern-free

CLOUD COMPUTING IS THE summation of a series of technologies that have been converging for a while. Today, cloud computing has become a solid option for organisations of all sizes but there are concerns still holding some back from moving things from theory to reality.

So what's the problem? Plenty, it would seem. Many of the concerns and issues are unique to industry sector and business size, but there are some common themes. Read on to discover the 10 main reasons people might be holding back on deploying cloud-based projects and services.

1

Infrastructure

Fast, reliable internet access is key. That's something that's quite easy to manage when the bulk of workers are in an office but it gets trickier with remote workers and those who travel.

Given that one of the main benefits of cloud working is to have access to files and applications wherever you happen to be, variable web access quality has to be a concern.

This applies equally to people accessing in-house computers over the internet. But when everyone in an organisation is dependent on a cloud platform, there is an understandable concern that there is no fall-back position for a vital part of a company's infrastructure – and one that underpins most other operations.

2

Losing control

It's not just an emotional attachment to a computer room that keeps companies from outsourcing. It's the fact they feel more secure by having data under close control.

Removing the need for local storage clearly has some cost benefits, but for a generation of system administrators and support staff brought up on a different way of working, it's a change that rings some alarm bells.

One is trusting an external source for working data – what happens if access drops or if someone loses the data? There's a leap of faith and an element of uncertainty that creeps in when data management is moved out of the immediate control of an IT department.

3

Fear of change

People do fear any sort of change, even in a fast moving industry such as IT. They don't tend to fear upgrades too much – although a jump say to the latest Microsoft Office can mean some firefighting – but a wholesale alteration in the way systems are supposed to work is a challenge.

It's hard not to have some empathy with this. In many organisations, IT is a tool, a means to do a job, and nothing more than that. There's a strong argument that the software industry, in particular, has become adept at selling upgrades and alterations that we don't actually need, or that don't make a difference to daily life. So when a change comes along that does, reticence is hardly surprising.

Persuading people to alter the way that they've done things for years, whether attempted via carrot or stick, is rarely a straightforward battle.

So persuading key decision makers and their staff to embrace cloud computing can be a heck of a job. Even the best-deployed cloud solution might therefore still be a bit of a bumpy ride (see also number 10 – the human factor).

4

Security

When data is being looked after by another party, it's right and proper that security issues are raised. Every business has confidential information that it likes to keep behind closed doors, and the fear that cloud computing could make such material more vulnerable isn't one that can simply be ignored.

Yet recent times have seen that the biggest source of confidential document leaks is more likely to have been a misplaced USB stick, using unsecured internet connections and less than honest employees.

Reputable cloud service providers view security as pivotal to what they offer and, with the added help of a bit of common sense, there's a strong argument that most businesses would benefit from more robust security if they do migrate to a cloud service.

5

Cloud outage

Clearly, this is a very real and sensible concern. There's no computer network in the world that doesn't have the risk of downtime at some point in its life. However, there's still the comfort blanket of being able to yell at an IT department and get up-to-the-minute information when it's a self-hosted computer network that's at the heart of the problem.

What happens, though, when that's taken out into a cloud environment? Who gets the ear-bashing then? And, more to the point, what happens when a cloud service a business is relying on goes down, even for a short period? With localised working, even without a network, having some machines with working productivity software installed at least means things can get done.

What's often forgotten in this argument, though, is that a cloud service stands a good chance of having a working, operational backup called into action quickly. Furthermore, one by-product of cloud adoption is that the maintenance and repair of problems is also outsourced, so it may well be that any problems are resolved faster than an in-house team can act.

Service providers should – and do – also have incentives to ensure maximum uptime.

6

Paying the bill

There are some obvious economic benefits to adopting cloud services, from a reduction in dependency on in-house IT, to the outsourcing of data management and security, and the saving, potentially, on expensive software licences, and battling to keep hardware performance up to date.

Yet the future is uncertain. Technology is littered with examples of new innovations and developments that were initially designed to reduce costs, and yet many business are still investing heavily in their IT budgets.

Some valid questions arise about cloud computing, then. Is it offering value for money? What guarantees are in place that pricing won't slide upwards as businesses become more and more dependant on cloud services? Is this just software companies trying to get us to switch to a subscription system for licences, and so the longer term cost may actually be higher?

These are appropriate questions, often with no immediate answer. There's an element of leap of faith, and a need to secure a good service contract. But cast iron guarantees? They're lacking at present, and for firms with razor-tight balance sheets that has to be an issue.

7

It's too early

Even accepting the comparable maturity of some elements of cloud-based working (many, for instance, trust their email to a webmail service with little worry), there remains a feeling, rightly or wrongly, that this is still an area of computing that's in its infancy. Let's not forget, too, that lots of 'next big things' have gone on to be anything but. As such, many businesses are holding back from adopting cloud services as they wait to see how the assorted offerings develop, and as they let others do the pathfinding for them.

There's always some sense to not moving business-critical operations to areas where you'd be an early adopter (although cloud adoption can, and should, be done piecemeal), and there's a feeling that the wrinkles need to be resolved in cloud services before more firms embrace the potential on offer.

Yet, there's a degree of obvious myth to the argument that the services are immature – after all, Salesforce.com has been around since 1999, an eternity in IT terms. Rather, we are more likely reacting to changes in the way services are packaged and sold, although there are clear reasons to be cautious if, say, the local internet infrastructure is rather poor and you want to invest in a public cloud system.

8

We are not lemmings

Much of the discussion surrounding cloud computing has implicit assumptions built into it. That it's the right thing to do. That it's the logical next step in business technology. That it's a question of when, rather than if, a company should take advantage of what cloud computing offers. In much the same way that it was once assumed that everybody would upgrade their copy of Windows within a couple of years of Microsoft releasing a new version, there's an impression sometimes put across that cloud computing will become compulsory.

But, of course, it isn't. There is doubt that the argument that cloud is the future has been convincingly made. Because, while there are potentially huge benefits to what's being offered, there's no one-size-fits-all mentality here. Is cloud computing really the right option for a small business of two or three people? Is it the right way forward for a large organisation, with hundreds of employees in many different locations?

There are strong cases to be made in both instances that the answer is yes (again, down to the fact that you can choose what works for you, with public, private and hybrid cloud approaches on offer). But that doesn't mean that the case doesn't have to be made.

The benefits of the cloud have to be defined, be tangible, and be presented properly. It's the users who tumble over the cliff to follow the crowd who will, inevitably, hit problems, and fail to reap the intended benefits of what the cloud can offer.

▶

9

What, actually, is it?

Arguably one of the biggest challenges facing cloud computing is this: how, exactly, do you define it? Because already, different service providers describe cloud products in very different ways. There doesn't appear to be one widely accepted definition of what cloud computing is, and without that, packaging and selling the benefits to organisations is made that bit more difficult.

Furthermore, part and parcel of the uncertainties surrounding cloud computing is the argument over standards. There's no solid, common and obvious foundation for cloud services to build on. Like it or lump it, people know where they are with a Windows operating system, a copy of Lotus Notes and some variant of an office suite. But what such common, unifying tools exist in the cloud? There are not, at this stage, obvious, dominant players in the market – although Amazon, Google and Salesforce.com would stake claims – and for companies looking for a big brand name to trust, that does have to come into their thinking.

Until cloud computing can be defined in a manner that's as understandable as an operating system or an office suite (and arguably, it can be defined as both), it's going to create some uncertainty within firms as to what exactly they're being sold, and how it allows them to work with others.

10

The human factor

At the heart of every significant problem to do with technology lies the same factor: people. We have seen time and time again that you can have an IT infrastructure that's seemingly tight and secure, but it's a simple human slip that's opened up an element of risk. Furthermore, someone who doesn't fully understand, or doesn't want to understand, what it is that they're being presented with, will always cause some degree of problem.

It may be straightforward to get the MD and finance director to sign off on the financial benefits, but just look at how hard it is to get 'buy-in' for end users to use systems such as CRM (customer relationship management). New web-based systems in the cloud may pose similar problems.

Realistically, of course, every issue we've discussed here has a person at the heart of it, or a fear of what someone can, and inevitably will do, when given the keys to something new and different (and that's just one individual: the potential dangers multiply exponentially when people hunt in packs).

It's a big problem, and why many businesses are keen to retain the technological status quo, in that it keeps the human–technology balance in a position that it's migrated to over a period of time.

It's important never to forget the 'people factor' when bringing in any new technology. ■

Don't miss out on the latest cloud news

Register for the Cloud Pro newsletter and you could be in with a chance of winning an Amazon Kindle Touch

Cloud Pro is the UK's definitive guide to all things cloud. Make sure you don't miss out on key cloud developments and announcements by signing up to the Cloud Pro newsletter. That way, cloud news and views will be delivered straight to your inbox without you having to do a thing.

Sign up today and you could be in with a chance of winning an Amazon Kindle Touch.*

Simply head to http://bit.ly/LlcWWT to register.

Cloud Pro Newsletter
20th June 2012

CloudPro

CLOUD ESSENTIALS | SOFTWARE AS A SERVICE | INFRASTRUCTURE AS A SERVICE | PLATFORM AS A SERVICE | PROVIDERS

Top News Stories

Google: Apps in the cloud are more eco-friendly
Google has claimed that companies could reduce energy costs by between 65 and 85 per cent simply by migrating from on-premise applications to Google Apps.

The search for the best in British cloud is on
The European cloud industry organisation, Eurocloud, is still looking for the top cloud

Dear Subscriber,

Welcome to the *Cloud Pro* newsletter for Wednesday 20th June 2012.

Once you've made the decision to move to the cloud, how should you deal with your cloud provider? More specifically, what should be in the contract - one manager gives his view of this tricky topic.

Competition ends 1st December 2012
* for full terms and conditions, please visit http://www.dennis.co.uk/comp/terms

Peering into the cloud crystal ball

The way we work will look very different in 10 or 20 years and cloud computing is going to drive much of that change

PREDICTING THE FUTURE is tough. Just ask Ethernet inventor Bob Metcalfe, who famously predicted the internet would collapse under the volume of traffic (and publicly had to eat his magazine column when it did no such thing). Or ask Bill Gates, who famously said spam would disappear within a couple of years.

Trying to predict the shape of the cloud market over the next five years or more, therefore, is not the simplest of tasks. A couple of years ago, analyst firm Gartner gazed into its crystal ball and stated 20 per cent of companies would have no IT department by the end of 2012. We are now staring that date in the face and we're a long way from that prophecy coming true.

We are far from Gartner's bold vision coming true – but that's no reason, just yet, for analysts to pull out their cutlery and tuck into the prediction.

There are plenty of indications that the move to cloud is set to continue apace. The value for public cloud services is expected to show a massive increase over the next four years: according to research company IDC, the market will grow from $21.5 billion in 2010 to $72.9 billion by 2015.

Cisco's June 2012 CloudWatch report found that cloud computing was on the agenda of 90 per cent of IT decision makers - up from the 52 per cent reported in 2011. Of this majority, almost a third (31 per cent) view cloud computing as critical.

What's more, of the companies surveyed confirming they had a cloud agenda, some 85 per cent said they were planning on making further investments in this area over the coming year.

The results make interesting reading when compared with the same Cisco study conducted in 2011. Cost reduction, for example, was cited then as fifth most important, whereas it claims the top spot in the 2012 research.

"It would seem, whichever way we look at things, the future is very bright. In fact, it's cloud shaped."

Why have we become so much more willing to adopt cloud services? There are

Cloud Computing

several reasons, including a growing understanding of what cloud means. Facebook users worldwide are used to the idea of applications being hosted elsewhere. The use of the word 'cloud' by Apple, Microsoft et al has probably helped, too.

There's also the way in which initial concerns have been dismissed. A major inhibitor used to be security potential customers were not happy about leaving data with a third party. There's now a growing acceptance that cloud service providers have a strong interest in keeping data safe and, what's more, have the infrastructure in place to do so.

Perhaps the biggest driver is the need for firms to be flexible and react more quickly to changing market conditions.

This is going to lead to some major changes:

- The cloud will spread rapidly in small businesses. We're already seeing this, but the trend will accelerate;
- Most software will be delivered via subscription – again, this is happening already;
- There will be a big shift to hybrid clouds as firms become much smarter about which applications they move to the cloud;

- Much more work will be done on identity management for improved access to cloud services while maintaining security;
- We'll see more community clouds. There are cloud platforms for different organisations with common interests and objectives. The most well-known UK example is the Government G-Cloud initiative. Others will follow;
- Accurate chargeback will be more prevalent as the IT time and usage of departments within organisations is more accurately measured;
- There will be changes in data centre location. The need to be near head office and areas of population will disappear. Latency will become less of an issue.

In the longer term, we could see employees working in small, local hubs housing 50 or 60 people, but shared between companies. You may be working in insurance, but sit next to someone working for a bookies and opposite someone working for a publisher.

Resources could be virtually allocated and, with greater use of video-conferencing and collaboration software, workers would be quickly connected to their peers.

It's a radical change, but current employment practices of commuting and working 9 to 5 have scarcely changed since Victorian times. It's unlikely this approach will last another 100 years.

Werner Vogels, Amazon Web Services' CTO, says, when it comes to cloud, we're still at Day One – a mark of how much change there is to come. Enterprises will look very different in 10 or 20 years and cloud computing is going to drive much of that change.

There are other work-related benefits too. Cloud computing has been heralded not just as the future for IT but also a saviour for the UK economy and something that will drive a host of new jobs.

In a study, commissioned by Microsoft, researchers at the London School of Economics (LSE) looked at the projected impact of cloud on the aerospace and smartphone industries to see just how much of an impact it could have on employment.

The Modelling the Cloud report – which focused on the UK, US, Germany and Italy - stated that investment in cloud computing had a direct and indirect effect on job creation in both industries, firstly through the construction and staffing of the data centres required for hosting the cloud services and, secondly, by freeing IT staff and other skilled employees to concentrate on other areas of work.

The LSE research also showed that an investment in cloud computing will not lead to any rise in unemployment as companies will be looking to hire new staff and, contrary to widespread belief, be looking to move and re-train existing employees. It's much more a case of boom and boom than doom and gloom, then.

However, the nature of the business also has an effect: the web-focused smartphone industry is expected to show a far higher growth rate than the aerospace business. The study predicts that between now and 2014, the number of cloud-related jobs in the UK smartphone sector will rise by 349 per cent. This compares with just 55 per cent growth in the aerospace market.

The report's authors, Jonathan Liebenau, Patrik Karrberg, Alexander Grous and Daniel Castro, wrote that the arrival of cloud services will be a useful driver for European growth. This is no doubt music to the ears of EU commissioner, Neelie Kroes, who has stressed the importance of cloud computing to the European economy. To harness this, the authors believe that policy makers should follow three guidelines.

- The provision of improved education and re-training in eSkills;
- Provision of incentives for companies to adopt green energy practices that can attract investment in the cloud, particularly in when it comes to data centre location;
- Ensuring data transfer policies, such as privacy rights protection, do not impede the development of cloud services.

Whichever way we look at things, the future is very bright. In fact, it's cloud shaped. ■

The shape of things to come

- Almost half (43 per cent) of users are adopting cloud services for flexibility;
- Cost savings are the driver for some 17 per cent;
- The low cost of adopting cloud services is the draw for 14 per cent;
- Almost three quarters (73 per cent) expect to increase cloud deployments in the next year;
- Email services (36 per cent), data storage (35 per cent), backup/DR (28 per cent), collaboration (28 per cent) and hosting (26 per cent) are the biggest areas likely to be migrated to the cloud;
- Data security (62 per cent), privacy (55 per cent), connectivity (49 per cent), confidence (35 per cent) and lock-in (34 per cent) are the biggest concerns relating to moving to the cloud.

SOURCE: CLOUD INDUSTRY FORUM CLOUD ADOPTION AND TRENDS FOR 2012 REPORT

How the cloud can make your business agile

This talk of technology is all very well, but the true potential of cloud computing lies in transforming your business with speed and collaboration

DOES ANYONE remember timesharing computers in universities? Or value-added networks (VANs) and electronic data interchange (EDI) in business trading networks? Or even insurance salespeople armed with Psion palmtop computers?

Many proponents of cloud computing act as though they've just discovered the kind of cloud-type business processes that organisations have, in fact, been tackling with various degrees of success for many years. These advocates also maintain that cloud is a technology-driven new wave that, while bringing new business opportunities, is mainly about scaling up infrastructure in data centres, with the obvious advantages of access to the latest technology, elimination of in-house servers and so on.

But the technology itself, while obviously vital, is really a sideshow to realising the business transformation efforts that enlightened organisations have been striving for over the last 20 years or so. As Walter Adamson, an Australian-based consultant, comments: "Clouds are about ecosystems, about large collections of interacting services including partners and third parties, about inter-cloud communication and sharing of information through such semantic frameworks as social graphs."

Transformation vs utility

This, he adds, is clearly business transformational, whereas "computing services that are delivered as a utility from a remote data centre" are not. The pioneers in VANS/EDI methods – which are now migrating into modern cloud systems in offerings from software firm SAP and its partners, for example – were able to set up basic trading data exchange networks, but the cloud transformation now is integrating, in real-time, the procurement, catalogue, invoicing and other systems across

possibly overlapping and much wider business communities.

Likewise, companies struggled for a long time with mobile and remote access to sales and marketing systems, as enterprise integration was often very difficult and expensive. Now the transformation brought about by cloud ecosystems such as the Salesforce.com community is enabling far more than a mobile quotation system with data that a rep had to download using a modem before he or she set out for the day.

And clearly, there are many individuals and companies, especially small firms, that have happily taken to one of the world's most complete cloud experiences, Amazon Web Services, which is enabling many to move from a static website to a fully-fledged online global shop, with everything from database management to micropayment handling. And Amazon is also a frontrunner in the enterprise 'private cloud', with major software vendors – including Oracle and SAP – now on its infrastructure offering.

But is that offering business agility beyond the IT side? The 2011 *Business Week* article 'The cloud: battle of the tech titans', looked at Amazon vs the rest and focused pretty much on the scale argument, with users renting server time to analyse sales data, for example. But it does note that time to market is a major pull.

The city of Miami, for example, quickly built a service that monitors non-emergency calls. "Local residents can go to a website that pulls up a map of the city and place pins in every spot tied to a complaint," it is claimed.

"Before the cloud, the city would have needed three months to develop a concept, buy new computing systems (including extras in case of a hurricane), get a team to install all the necessary software, and then build the service."

Such systems are unlikely to be built in the 'conventional' way in these cash-strapped days.

Sandwich course

Food chain EAT is another good example of private cloud user, this time Google Apps. The company is using Google Talk to improve business processes by sending instant messages between stores when, for example, one run outs of a popular sandwich. Google Forms are also being use by head office to survey shop managers to capture issues and ideas, and integration with smartphones, for managers to access documents and order stocks on the move, and to oversee ▶

"Larry Ellison famously cracked the whip a few years ago when he realised he had no dashboard to see what his business units were doing."

a number of restaurants while being stationed at one.

The received wisdom about such business cloud applications is that vendors are approaching business department heads, not IT managers, to make sales, although not much enterprise software of any type has been sold this way since the dot-com crash.

It certainly makes sense in one of the hardest functions to crack, the salesforce, which has long put up resistance to clunky CRM systems foisted on them. Just because Salesforce.com's CRM system is cloud-based does not mean it does not have the adoption problems that CRM has suffered from – incentives and good management tend to fix that. But a cloud system can greatly help with business change in hard to reach parts of a firm.

In many companies there is a black hole of forecasting and pipeline data on sales, and it doesn't help that most major enterprises – certainly in the FTSE 100 – are led by CEOs with little or no sales experience. It's an area tailor-made for the cloud since so much knowledge is in silos – around departments and in the heads of salespeople – and best practice is not shared.

Fast forward for sales

Phil Codd, chief markets officer for northern Europe at software testing firm SQS, chose Salesforce.com to solve a major sales reporting problem – in the past, reporting was on an individual country basis with a complex mix of spreadsheets, emails and word of mouth which placed a lot of pressure on accurate and timely sales forecasting.

Codd took advantage of Salesforce.com's 30-day free trial of its Sales Cloud 2, and then worked with consultancy SaasPoint to implement it in just 40 working days. The company now has a central, real-time repository of its sales pipeline throughout the region, in addition to all sorts of new opportunities for sharing sales best practice and leads via tools such as Salesforce.com's internal social media system, Chatter.

Anything that produces more than the sum of a notoriously self-sufficient group of reps is more than useful and it's hard to underestimate what this can do for a company.

Larry Ellison, the colourful boss of software giant Oracle and now a cloud convert, famously cracked the whip a few years ago when he realised he had no 'dashboard' to see what his business units were doing in a timely fashion round the world – and got it done, of course.

In-house not an option

Trying to build an in-house system to do this is obviously counter-productive in time and money for most companies that are not of the likes of Oracle.
Where Salesforce.com also scores is in its brilliant decision to create the AppExchange platform where users can integrate and use many more functions, from an 800-long list, and that's apart from Salesforce's own extras.

Another function that's benefiting from cloud 'agility' is logistics, where provider Deltion is gaining a good deal of success for its CarrierNet platform. Managing director Denis O'Sullivan, himself a logistics expert brought in to run this UK firm a year ago, says logisticians have been 'crying out' for a long time for real-time visibility across the supply chain to iron out customer service problems, which he says Cadbury (now

Enterprise cloud means business agility

PricewaterhouseCoopers (PwC) recommends the following:

1. Start by knowing where the organisation stands on the cloud computing continuum. Use benchmarking and gap analysis to understand where you are today;
2. Conceptualise and communicate a compelling vision for using cloud computing to advance business objectives;
3. Develop a cloud strategy and execution plan that incorporates any ad hoc components implemented already and lays out a systematic approach to moving forward;
4. Understand the goal, which is not to get to cloud computing, but to achieve ever-greater levels of business efficiency and agility;
5. Progress systematically through the five levels* of cloud computing components, realising that not all components are appropriate in all situations;
6. Balance the use of private and public clouds to form a hybrid cloud that draws on both private and public cloud resources as needed;
7. Focus on automation, which is the key to efficiency, agility and scalability.

* SET OUT IN PWC'S PAPER, 'CLOUDS IN THE ENTERPRISE: NAVIGATING THE PATH TO BUSINESS ADVANTAGE', AVAILABLE AT WWW.PWC.COM

part of Kraft) is doing with CarrierNet, a cloud system.

Keith Newton, customer logistics director at Cadbury says: "The implementation has enabled us to move from a series of unlinked systems to a web based interfaced solution that has totally eliminated a number of areas of failure. It links all internal logistics and planning teams at Cadbury, all tier one third party logistics service providers, all second tier hauliers subcontracted to them, and customers via alerts, SMS and emails. "It is no coincidence that since implementation we have recorded a number of '100 per cent customer service days', which is a significant achievement for a large FMCG firm such as Cadbury."

For which read if the truck breaks down and no one knows, the kids don't get their chocolate. O'Sullivan adds that large retailers are also in the market for his system – which again would be prohibitive now to try and build in-house – and also mentions a client called Rigid Plastic Containers (RPC) which uses CarrierNet to check warehouse stock and production schedules before processing transport orders. If there is no warehouse stock, the system checks if the ordered items will be produced in time for despatch. If there is a potential problem, an exception alert is raised and the problem managed with the customer.

Logistics examples are significant because they often involve the ecosystems that promote more business transformation across partners – adding real-time bidding systems to take on jobs, for example, is another feature O'Sullivan mentions that a client is doing. An ecosystem also becomes apparent within companies as they use cloud systems for human resources.

In some cases, it is certainly the case that cloud technology creates a new business agility opportunity. In others, it's enabling better a known need. Donald Rumsfeld had a good take on this… ■

Board-level priorities for cloud

We take a tour through the top board jobs affected by what for many will be a major business change in the years ahead

CLOUD COMPUTING WAS unheard of as a term before 2007. In just five years it has risen from marketing shorthand to become the symbol of a massive change in technology.

What makes cloud computing different is that it's a technological change that touches on every part of the business. For the finance director there are changes in the way IT services are bought; sales managers have a new way to communicate and interact with their teams and customers; the IT director will find his or her budget, strategy and team transformed. Above all, the CEO will have to think about the way his or her entire organisation is structured.

In the future, we could be talking about a complete overhaul of the way companies are constructed, about how they consume IT, about how their accounting works and, indeed, where they're located.

But those changes mean different things to different parts of the business. If we look at the way cloud services impact on different job roles, we can see that they're going to approach these changes in very different ways.

For the finance director/CFO

Perhaps the biggest driver for the move to cloud is the need to reduce costs, but that move works on many levels.

The change that has garnered most publicity is the move from counting IT as a capital expenditure to an operational one. Although often cited as a reason to move from on-premise hosting to cloud, this is somewhat misleading. What's really at stake is cash flow; by going down the cloud route, customers no longer have to commit to large costs up front. It isn't necessarily true to say that it's always going to be cheaper, but there are other advantages. ▶

There may even be a price premium in opting for cloud, but that needs to be set aside for other considerations. The price of renting a server could initially appear to cost more than purchasing, but the finance director has to consider the cost of power and cooling, the cost of staff, the maintenance costs, accounting for backup and disaster recovery and various other costs.

There's also the fact it's no longer necessary to be so rigorous about capacity planning – that becomes a headache for the cloud provider, not your IT director – and companies will be more flexible about installing new services and scaling up and down.

This is an important aspect. Previously, the IT department would have installed an infrastructure that could handle the peaks of the business. This was always a grossly inefficient way of organising IT services. It could be an infrastructure that is geared up to handle peaks of traffic – perhaps around the end of financial quarters, or around Christmas for retailers.

"Now there's a real way of measuring just how much computing time the marketing department has used."

But those brief periods of intense activity would have an effect on IT provision for the entire year. It's not too unlike a family of four opting for a minibus purely to cope with the yearly visit of the cousins who lived abroad. Cloud computing changes all that. Indeed, for the first time, organisations will no longer have to plan for the periods of greatest demand.

Coupled with this will be a change of practice when it comes to allocating departmental costs. Finance directors will now have an accurate way of deciding which costs are set against which department. This is a fundamental shake-up: even companies that have charge back to separate departments have often found this is little more than an estimate of a share of the costs. Managers have few tools to assess a real cost and have derived a figure from a combination of real figures and informed guesses.

Now there's a real way of measuring just now much computing time the marketing department has used, how much storage the graphics department has grabbed and the bandwidth needs of finance.

That capability, however, could lead to some finely tuned judgment. When departments' real costs are assessed accurately there could be some resentment from those that have been undercharged in earlier years and now

find their costs increasing (or resentment from departments that have been overcharged for several years). Either way, the finance director is likely to act as the diplomat smoothing over territorial disputes, ensuring the winners don't get triumphant and the losers don't become embittered.

"Managers have few tools to assess a real cost and have derived a figure from a combination of real figures and informed guesses."

Another key area the finance director must keep tabs on is licensing. Many vendors have not yet grasped the transformational nature of cloud computing and their licensing models are not able to cope with this new paradigm. The finance director, in conjunction with the IT head, needs to assess the state of licensing within the organisation, making sure that the company isn't overpaying.

The thorniest problem of all will be the negotiation and monitoring of the service level agreements (SLAs) with cloud providers. While the IT director will probably remain the best person to check on service delivery, the finance director will need some understanding of the potential level of financial loss suffered and the possible levels of compensation. This is a crucial area for the move to cloud computing: delivery to this sort of model will never work if the cloud provider can't provide the desired level of service and if the customer is under-compensated.

Ever since cloud computing emerged as a new catchphrase for the IT world, there have been several vendors leaping on to the bandwagon and 'cloud washing' existing products to suggest a strong commitment to the cloud. There are some finance directors or IT directors who may be tempted to follow the same path and 'cloud wash' their IT department. These instances will probably be rare but there's certainly been resistance to the idea of cloud computing from some IT department chiefs and the finance director may find himself as some sort of cloud arbiter.

The stakes are high for businesses. It will be a rare company that relies entirely on in-house IT in future. Some companies will move entirely to the cloud, some will move part of their infrastructure, some will move nothing. It's a decision that's going to require some careful assessment of the pros and cons and the finance director will play a vital role in assessing the financial rationale. ▶

For the IT director

IT directors have a different path to cloud. They have been aware of the debate and some of the buzzwords: public cloud; private cloud; SaaS; outsourcing; cloud-sourcing; crowd-sourcing. But, unusually, these terms are just as likely to have come from the board as from the IT side.

For once, the majority of hardcore techies and their sources have underplayed the significance of cloud. This is partly because it's perceived as a threat – outsource services and you'll surely lose part of your team, is the thinking – but also because for them it's an emergent set of trends in virtualisation and hosting: a confection, made out of pre-existing components with the key innovations happening several years ago.

This makes the balance of emails hitting inboxes of IT directors all the stranger; a vast number of people, with salespeople in the vanguard, are attaching the word cloud to their sales pitches as if it's their road to personal salvation. In this new world the cloud is the outsourcing industry's wholehearted attack on the massive budgets and imposing empires of corporate IT. That's why less tech-savvy board colleagues love it so much. It isn't easy for an IT director to reject all these overtures.

Among the ambitious PowerPoint presentations there will be a quiet voice from a clever guy who promises to chop your re-investment costs by 75 per cent, without moving a corporate data set outside your building. That last guy is talking about private clouds, which is the data centre, virtualised and shrunk, and made mobile (in the sense that it can move from one compute host to another, and nothing at all to do with the iPhone).

IT directors who get drawn into an early-adopter, single-purpose cloud-badged project could find themselves in great difficulty if they don't check details carefully. This is because the momentum of the optimistic, ignorant and misguided can be an astonishing thing, and because the hosting business has very little in the way of verification, standards, agreed procedures, or compensation packages for the day when something goes rather amiss. Hosting underpins cloud, and also wage packets if the IT director bets the company's operations on it.

Cloud companies that don't present rational means of running their services when their own platforms are offline are scarcely credible to seasoned technologists – so you have to be able to say, "What happens when it does not work?"

The answer lies with a private cloud. If sales teams are expected to do thousands of deals a day on an externally hosted service, then replicating that data internally on a compatible virtualisation platform is an insurance policy against not just kit failure at the SaaS provider but also the sudden loss of your own internet connection, perhaps traced to a telco's engineering works in the street outside.

In all likelihood, the eventual impact of cloud concepts will be somewhat less than the hopeful CEO – dreaming of losing his entire IT department – currently thinks. But it will also be a lot greater than the scornful nerd, looking at the toolbox cloud uses for delivery and finding nothing new or clever about it, is currently able to foresee.

It's also possible for an IT director to be in a business so secure, or so closely tied to physical processes, or so hugely dependent on a specific and ancient software suite, that there's no chance of making use of the high-profile parts of cloud computing. Companies running a factory floor of milling machines, or a metro line full of ticket readers, will find it difficult to run an on-demand capacity expansion project.

"IT directors who get drawn into an early-adopter, single-purpose cloud-badged project could find themselves in great difficulty."

What the IT director does find difficult is to show that cloud computing has been assessed as a possibility. There will be a lot of pressure on them from less 'techie' board members and it's important that the cloud option has been thoroughly investigated and, if ruled out, done so for the right reasons.

For the chief executive

The modern CEO isn't going to be short of advice in his attempt to get up-to-speed with cloud computing. But many of the opinions will be proffered by a host of vendors, cloud providers and channel partners – all of which will have their own agenda.

So, where does the CEO look to get the best advice on a move to the cloud? There are some things to focus on at the highest level, which lower-level managers and 'direct reports' won't necessarily have at the forefront of their minds. Terminology is one of those things. Your irritation at technical types babbling away using terms they don't define, no matter how well-intended you can see they are, gets some real teeth when it comes to cloud topics. There are a multitude of definitions out there, so how do you sort out which is best?

The top priority for any CEO contemplating a move to the cloud is to check the small print as if your life depends on it – because it could be that your business will come to depend on it. If you're unsure, consult with lawyers.

Cloud is about delivery of services and ensuring that cloud providers meet with their responsibilities.

Research by Queen Mary College in 2010 revealed a wide disparity of wording within cloud computing contracts. This is one area where the small print is not to be ignored as the contract will be the basis for the way that the company runs – indeed it could be crucial to whether the company survives or not if things don't go quite to plan.

What happens when a cloud provider is hit by a denial-of-service attack? What stops a provider from moving data to another jurisdiction for cost or legal reasons? Is the provider the definitive provider-of-last-resort, or is it just ▶

Does the CIO have a future in this new cloud-based world?

It is wrong to think the changes brought about by cloud will result in the demise of the IT leader. On-demand technology offers IT leaders opportunities to concentrate on real value-adding activities, such as strategy and innovation.

"If anything, cloud computing is more likely to strengthen the CIO role," says Ian Cox, a CIO who recently left infrastructure specialist May Gurney after four years as IT director. "Cloud offers CIOs the opportunity to reposition themselves within their organisations and increase their chances of expanding their influence and remit."

The cloud, then, actually represents good news for the CIO. Rather than allocating 80 per cent of their time and budget to operational IT concerns, CIOs have the opportunity to think about how to embed the cloud as part of a long-term business technology strategy that delivers innovation.

reselling someone else's package? What happens if a customer wants to move providers or go back to in-premise? Due diligence isn't just a tick box in taking up services in the cloud, it's a major component of the project time.

The next question for an organisation to consider is how closely it wants to work with its cloud provider. Some will be hands-off and see themselves as a facility for handling peak demands. Some will be more personal and try to be intimately involved in their customers' business.

Be wary though: the dream of many of the upsellers in the current wave of cloud hype is to pretend to be removable, when in fact they fully intend to hook customers for the foreseeable future.

Keeping independence is very much a CEO-level question, as is the exit strategy. Cloud is meant to be all about steering work to an available resource, not watching it vanish behind someone else's security gates.

Cloud computing presents the CEO with a major opportunity to reshape and reorganise their business. It's not just about technology either. Indeed, it's about how to use, analyse and improve company data and it's about using IT to have a positive impact on business processes.

Many companies have operated on the 'we've always done things this way' principle – cloud computing will offer the opportunity to do away with this thinking.

The world of cloud represents a step away from how we do things now and, of course, how we used to do things. But that change doesn't have to be a negative one if tackled in the right way and for the right reasons.

While cloud computing may not be for every business or every CEO, every one should at least be looking at the technology to see if/how/where it fits into their business model both now and in the future.

In the future, the best companies - on all sides of the cloud fence - will be those where the board looks at the direction the organisation is headed over the next five years and the best means of getting there.

If that involves cloud computing in any shape or form, now is most certainly the best time to be thinking about it. After all, if you're not, your competitors surely will be. ■

CASE STUDY

Private Cloud
OVH

vmware vCLOUD POWERED

Launch your projects instantly with Private Cloud

Private Cloud allows you to reduce deployment time and thus improve efficiency

Based on VMware solutions, OVH Private Cloud allows rapid deployment: in a few minutes, a Private cloud built according to the company's criteria and needs can be provisioned. If you feel the need to expand your business, you can benefit from the Private cloud by scaling the resources almost instantly.

The need: Provide a flexible and scalable virtualised infrastructure. In case of growth, businesses need to react quickly, without investing in new hardware.

The Private Cloud solution: The infrastructure management is simplified: the customer can add as many resources as necessary on the fly, without service interruption. Because all tasks are automated, a virtual machine configured according to specific needs can be made available in a few minutes.

Impact: A Microsoft Exchange platform based on PCC allows you to implement functional e-mail accounts for one, one hundred or one thousand customers in a few minutes.

OVH: What were your requirements?

Neil: We had to launch an email account service on a Microsoft Exchange platform for our customers. The aim was to offer them both a Private and Manager solution. Each customer would be provided with a dedicated virtual machine, which could evolve over time according to their needs. Regarding our global infrastructure, it had to be flexible! Because the number of customers was likely to increase, we'd need to be able to adapt our service to cope with this.

OVH: How has OVH met your expectations and requirements?

Neil: At first we were using other Cloud platforms. We were very happy with virtualisation, but we needed to balance and develop the infrastructure ourselves, we were not able to perform these operations instantly, which was synonymous with downtime for our customers. Whereas with the OVH Private Cloud we were able to automate these tasks. And with the SDK it was easy to plan maintenance and administration operations.

OVH: What has it changed for you?

Neil: Virtualisation is a revolution in itself, but we knew it already. Private Cloud has changed our life by allowing us to add servers on the fly. We don't have any more material issues, we can get many server configurations within a few clicks, some with extremely high performance! And the industrialisation process are simplified to the maximum. If our service works for two customers, it will work equally well for ten, thousand or even a million customers!

Cloud and SMEs – A perfect combination

Small organisations are obvious candidates for cloud computing, but there's still an awareness issue and SMEs should tread carefully

CLOUD COMPUTING IS an unusual phenomenon in the IT world as it is being used equally by small businesses and enterprises. Indeed, it's the smaller businesses that should benefit most as they are the companies that tend not to have large IT departments. Some small companies have no IT departments at all and are serviced by someone doing the job in his spare time, or by a local services company.

This is not the norm when it comes to technology. The natural order of things is for IT advances to start off in large businesses and work their way downwards: mobile phones started as an executive toy, now everyone has one; routers were part of the arcane global telecoms world, now people are connected at home.

Cloud computing has been different – there are many instances of SMEs adopting cloud-based delivery wholeheartedly, while larger enterprises have hesitated. Indeed, Andy Burton of the UK's Cloud Industry Forum believes that cloud computing is the first case of a technology that started in small businesses and has moved to larger ones.

Is the UK lagging behind?

But that's not the complete picture. In reality things are not entirely rosy for the cloud and SMEs. There have been some very enterprising small businesses who have been happy to adopt cloud as the backbone of their IT set-up but there's also a good deal of scepticism.

A survey in 2011 revealed some of this hesitancy. According to VMware, a provider of virtualisation software, only 48 per cent of British SMEs had begun using cloud technology. While this looks encouraging, the same survey found that 60 per cent of small businesses across Europe were going down this path. Other surveys have found even larger gaps in adoption and one reported that 43 per cent of SME respondents didn't even know what the term meant.

There are two problems with this: for a start, there are millions of people who are happily using consumer cloud services, such as Facebook and Google Mail, not to mention commercial cloud applications such as Google Apps and various smartphone apps. Second, figures from analyst IDC have shown that small businesses do not appear to be miserly when it comes to cloud – £9.8 billion was spent on cloud technologies in 2009 and half the figure came from SME budgets, it reports.

The seeming gap between the perception of cloud and expenditure can almost certainly be explained by a lack of

"Cloud computing is thought to be the first case of a technology that started in small businesses and has moved to larger ones."

understanding of what cloud is. There's a good chance that business people are using cloud services – even if they don't actually know it.

Software: the choice is yours

The other issue is that small companies tend not to be burdened with large legacy systems or have equipment that needs to be integrated in a cloud service. That's not to say that some do not have bespoke applications and specialist computer kit that may take time to phase out.

But if you're operating a start-up, there is little need to run any sort of IT facilities at all. By opting for Google Apps or Microsoft's new Office 365 cloud suite, a business could have all its productivity software (word processing, calendar, email and so on) working in the cloud. The business could also use accountancy software such as KashFlow to run its financials, Salesforce.com to handle its customer relationships and any number of software packages to look after its HR, marketing and procurement.

Higher up the scale, NetSuite offers cloud ERP (enterprise resource planning) software – the type of package that's normally the preserve of large businesses. In fact, just about every aspect of a modern day business could be run on ▶

cloud-based software.

And it's not just new cloud vendors that are providing options for these companies: plenty of long-established software firms are now in on the act. Accountancy software specialist Sage has released its own cloud-based software, ERP specialist SAP has taken its first steps down the cloud route and Oracle is embracing the technology, despite CEO Larry Ellison's initially dismissive remarks about cloud.

The most remarkable transformation of all has been Microsoft, which is a mainstay for so many small organisations in all sectors of the economy. The company's reputation has been built on boxed products and its licensing methodology had been geared towards this. But, in 2010, Microsoft's CEO, Steve Ballmer, said that the company was betting its future on the cloud. Since then it has looked to turn that vision into reality.

Office 365 is its step in that direction although Microsoft, unlike Google, its rival in the productivity suite stakes, has not quite managed to divorce itself from its roots and Office 365 does require some access to elements such as Exchange, SharePoint and Lync. Google does offer a 100 per cent cloud-based, standalone product with Google Apps, which many companies are turning to – although the company did lose some popularity when it reduced the number of users supported in its free version from 50 to 10.

A picture of what smaller companies are adopting when it comes to the cloud comes from US industry association CompTIA, which in a 2011 survey reported that storage and backup solutions are the most heavily used cloud applications (71 per cent of SMEs using the cloud), followed by email (62 per cent), document management (59 per cent), collaboration (56 per cent) and customer relationship management (53 per cent). Around a third of SMEs are using cloud services, and 92 per cent say their experience has been positive or very positive.

"Microsoft's CEO, Steve Ballmer, said that the company was betting its future on the cloud."

Key issues for small businesses

- Start small and build up – don't overprovision;
- The PAYG ethos is helpful but keep an eye on costs. PAYG can work out more expensive than on-premise so be sensible in your planning;
- Have a proper back-up and disaster recovery process in place. If something can go wrong, it will;
- Make sure you're buying services from a reputable supplier – there is a lot of 'cloud washing' (i.e. deceptive marketing) out there;
- You're still responsible for compliance. Don't pass the buck when it comes to conforming to regulations.

Counting on cost savings

It's not just the availability of heaps of software that's attractive to small businesses. There are also financial benefits. One of the biggest problems facing start-ups is cashflow, and the onset of cloud has reduced the cost of getting off the ground significantly in the last decade. The arrival of cloud has also made it easier to plan – financial forecasting becomes easier – and paying for services is now simpler. There are no more visits to the bank manager trying to argue about credit arrangements: a whole IT infrastructure can be arranged by the judicious use of the company credit card.

But not only that, there's no longer a need to guess what computer resources are needed: a company owner can now afford to start small and build up after the revenue has come in.

Having made the decision to go with cloud, the next stage is to work out the hardware: if you're not going to run with a server under your desk or tucked away in a corner somewhere, you're going to need a cloud service provider. Again, there are a host of providers to choose from, ranging from those who will provide you with your own remote server or a virtual server (that is, one dedicated to you or shared with other companies in a public cloud).

The company that really kick-started the cloud ethos for small organisations is Amazon. It realised that it had a large amount of under-used IT resources and started selling some of its spare computing and storage capacity. Amazon Web Services now has a massive share of the market. In August 2011, the company announced its cloud division was now a billion dollar business in its own right. It offers a range of cloud products but its main ones are EC2 (Elastic Compute Cloud) and S3 (Simple Storage Service), both of which are widely used by small businesses around the world.

Beware the small print

While it sounds like it could be a perfect match, there are still issues for SMEs to consider. Regardless of the size of the contract, it's still essential to get it checked to ensure that it covers all possibilities.

Companies would have more peace of mind if vendors had some form of certification: the UK's Cloud Industry Forum offers a self-certified code of practice that several companies (including Microsoft) have signed up to. Alternatively, there's a more rigorous offering in the pipeline under the banner of another industry organisation, Eurocloud. The Eurocloud Star Assessment accreditation scheme is not self-certified and costs the vendor a lot more to attain.

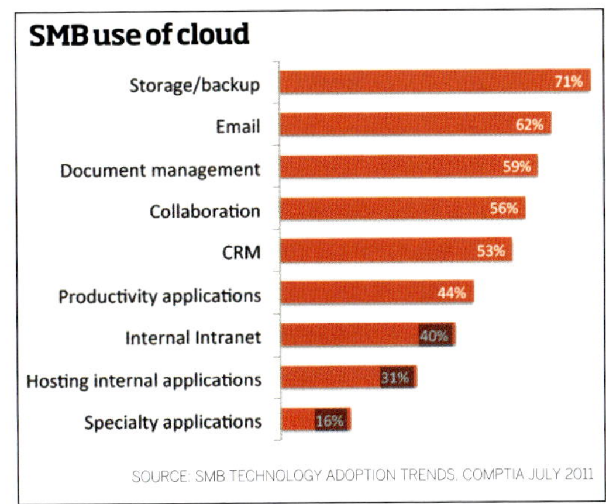

After checking the provenance of a cloud supplier, the details of its contract, formulating a disaster recovery plan and provisioning the initial services, then a company is ready to go. Many SMEs will have used a reseller to handle this part of the business, in which case it's important to know what after-sales plans are in place. Many resellers have been suspicious of cloud but the good ones know that it presents a new opportunity and are ready to meet the challenge – a helpful reseller will be invaluable in this process.

SMEs and cloud computing are a natural fit. Even if they don't always realise it. There may be some hesitancy but we're going to see most small organisations turn to the cloud in the future. ■

Those who have opted for the cloud need to be aware of some of the issues in the small print of the contract. Forewarned is forearmed

CLOUD CONTRACTS: Small print matters

ANYONE WHO'S BEEN TO a trade show will know that many a salesman will promise the earth when it comes to selling a service. However, the reality of the offering doesn't really always live up to those claims. There is often a disconnect between what's promised and what's actually delivered.

Sometimes sales brochures will contain phrases that appear to say one thing but often mean quite another to the cloud provider keen to have something to fall back on when trouble strikes.

Marketing hype vs reality

Faced with the glossy marketing literature what key phrases and watchwords should you be on the look out for? The ones that may appear innocuous at the time but whose double meaning can prove problematical when dealing with the day-to-day running of a cloud service for your users.

Cloud outages are very real. While cloud providers acknowledge these events can and do happen, there will be certain assurances within the marketing literature that these are rare events. While no-one can and does guarantee 100 per cent uptime, there are guarantees of 99.99 per cent and sometimes 99.999 percent (the so-called "five nines") within the prospectus. Often such statements are accompanied by the cover-all phrase "uptime cannot be guaranteed".

That said, cloud service providers do have some levels of service to stick to. There's a problem though: while failure to meet this criteria should result in compensation for lost productivity according to any service level ▶

agreements put in place, it is often the case that the rules are stacked against the end-user.

Indeed, not all instances are covered despite the wording in the prospectus implying that they will be, according to Keith Bates, chairman of the Cloud Computing Centre.

"We must question just how likely it is that a customer will ever receive a payout," he says. "It is, after all, no great secret that while SLAs look good for the customer on paper, they are always designed to work in favour of the service provider."

Downtime differences

Two scenarios can happen where the amassed downtime may or may not result in compensation. The first one is when a customer experiences continuous service downtime of 20 minutes, leaving them unable to access their email account, applications or data. Productivity is reduced; meaning business-critical work is lost. This customer is compensated as continuous downtime of 20 minutes in a single day breaks the agreed 99.99 per cent continuous uptime SLA in their contract.

> **"It is often the case that the rules are stacked against the end user."**

A second customer, however, experiences downtime of five minutes for four days in a row, meaning they are unable to access their email account, applications or data, disrupting the productivity and damaging the business on four separate occasions. This time, even though the total was 20 minutes downtime, the customer receives no compensation as this 20 minutes was not continuous. It pays to look past the sales talk and see just how rigorous the SLAs say they are in the brochure.

Another phrase to look out for is "customer support available 24/7". This may mean one thing to the customer, but can mean something quite different to the provider.

"Many 24/7 data centres [only] have a security guard on duty overnight, who will answer the phone," says Ray Welsh, head of marketing at secure data centre provider The Bunker, adding

others may have email-only service desk contact.

Potential customers should ask about technical support available throughout the week and for changes made to the service provided, issue resolution and so on, Welsh advises.

It is also important to realise that even when the appropriate support staff are available around the clock, if a major problem occurs and they are all out fixing problems when you raise a support call, you will almost certainly not get your issue fixed until they become available again. The business user has to ensure that any mission-critical services running from the cloud have the necessary staff on hand to deal with urgent problems there and then to stem the loss of productivity.

In reality, such contract phrases can all too often mean that the company accepts support requests 24/7 but you'll have to wait at least until the support staff arrive at their desks in the morning.

While cloud has lots of benefits and is indeed very flexible, that flexibility is limited. Unless a CIO signs up for a generic service and compromises on some requirements, they will need to identify a cloud service that meets the organisation's needs for various attributes.

"It's like buying car insurance," said Welsh.

"You need to find the provider that specialises in supplying a service tailored to your needs otherwise you won't get good value for money."

For example, attributes of a cloud service include: the degree and frequency of elasticity, amount of data segregation, provisioning time and who does this, security of the service and costs. The cheapest solution is unlikely to be the most secure and vice versa.

Contracts summary

Here's a quick checklist when it comes to contracts:

- Evaluate how much you're willing to pay to ensure your move to the cloud doesn't end up losing you money, or your business;
- Review the level of service from the provider. Does it provide adequate protection?
- Take appropriate steps – through your provider or otherwise – to ensure you have a disaster recovery plan that works;
- Consider what the provider is liable for and what has been excluded. Is this an acceptable level of risk?

Probing questions

The grand claim of "It is secure" should be one phrase that sounds a massive warning to any potential customer. Of course, many cloud providers make sure they offer the best security they know they can provide. But it is the customer's job to question the security set-up in depth.

What steps are taken to make the vendor's cloud service secure? How much of the infrastructure is shared and what steps are taken to segregate user data/processing/network? Who has access to each part of the infrastructure? What types of other customers are using this cloud and what associated risk profile do they bring? The security questionnaire should be the one that has the most questions that need to be answered.

Some have dressed up hosted IT services as cloud. This "cloudwash" means that often the prospectus offers a lot, but in the cold light of day it is nothing more than any hosted data centre service that has been around long before cloud was conceptualised. ■

CONTRACTS what to focus on

Frank Jennings, a senior partner at DMH Stallard, gives an overview of the main areas to consider when entering into a cloud computing deal

ONCE YOU'VE DECIDED to move away from computer systems that are physically located within your organisation, there's another problem to solve, and that's the contract you need to have with a provider.

The type of contract that you have with the cloud provider (or a reseller of the cloud provider's service) is key. Get this part wrong and your business could be looking at some serious financial and other consequences.

There are three main areas to concentrate on: reliability, security and liability, and you should be paying keen attention to a cloud provider's policy on all of them.

Is it reliable?

Reliability is about the technical performance of the cloud provider's service. Do their servers go down? What mirroring options do they have in place? What monitoring systems do they have in place? You should be prepared to carry out due diligence on the cloud companies and assess their performance. Look at the company's past history – does it have a good reputation?

On the other hand, cloud companies may point out that having an IT infrastructure in-house does not necessarily mean that your servers or network are more reliable. They will say that managing data centres is their core business and will claim that they're much better at managing this infrastructure than user organisations.

However, while it's true that cloud providers will tend to have more robust and better-managed infrastructures, you need more reassurance than that. It's vital that all the fine details are built into the service. And the type of cloud provider is important here – one factor to bear in mind is that buying a standard package from a larger operator will leave very little room to manoeuvre, while customising an offering from a smaller reseller could offer a more flexible experience.

Be secure

There are a couple of factors to consider when it comes to security. If you are in financial services you have to conform with the Financial Services Act and all companies will have to consider the Data Protection Act and the scrutiny of the Information Commissioner. Offending organisations can be hit by big fines: the FSA fined HSBC £3 million for losing data, for example.

To be blunt, the liability for any breaches of security or privacy lies with you – so you need to be concerned with the consequences of handing over information to a third party. It's very important to ensure that cloud providers are taking proper steps to protect data. Are they keeping it in the EU, as they're legally obliged to do, rather than sending it further afield? Some insist that UK data is housed in the UK – that's not legally necessary but it does give added peace of mind.

Although you as the customer are ultimately liable, there are steps that can be taken. You must include in the contract where the data is held and who it can be released to. There should also be an indemnity clause that stipulates that the cloud provider has taken all possible precautions to avoid security breaches and takes legal responsibility for any losses.

"Liability for any breaches of security lies with you. Be concerned about the consequences of handing data to a third party."

Ultimately, however, market forces will come into play. If a company loses data, then its reputation will suffer – cloud companies are going to stand or fall by their reliability and a few security breaches will quickly destroy that.

Who is liable?

The third factor to look at is liability – what happens when things go wrong with the day-to-day service? Levels of compensation need to be placed in the contract, but money will be of little satisfaction to a customer that has gone bust.

Some cloud providers try to exclude liability, rather in the same way that insurance companies will look not to pay out on their policies – although you could get around this by taking out your own insurance.

Another option is that cloud providers will offer some sort of protection but this will involve paying a higher fee for a gold or platinum service. This could mean that the cloud company is offering a more robust service, say at a high quality data centre with better monitoring facilities. Or it could be ▶

IN DEPTH: top nine contract areas to watch

Analyst firm Gartner suggests the following contract issues to consider when signing up with a cloud computing provider:

1. **Uptime guarantees** – Gartner says it has seen many contracts that have no uptime or performance service-level guarantees;
2. **Service-level agreement (SLA) penalties** – these should be financial and ideally money-back and not credits;
3. **SLA penalty exclusion** – look carefully at exclusions to penalties, such as ensuring a downtime calculation starts exactly when the downtime starts;
4. **Security** – Gartner says the provider's security practices should be at the same level as, or exceed, your own practices, especially for national privacy-related regulations. It recommends negotiating SLAs for security breaches;
5. **Business continuity and disaster recovery** – contracts rarely contain any provisions for disaster recovery, says Gartner, and some providers take no action to back-up customer data. You should ensure there is access to your own back-up measures where necessary;
6. **Data privacy conditions** – no personal data sharing should take place but contracts can be complex where there are multiple suppliers (e.g. both a software and platform provider is used);
7. **Suspension of service** – best to have an agreement that payments in any current legitimate dispute should not lead to a suspension of service;
8. **Termination** – provider contracts often have 30 day termination clauses. Look to extend this where possible;
9. **Liability** – Gartner recommends aiming for better liability protection than just a return of yearly fees.

SOURCE: IT PROCUREMENT BEST PRACTICE: NINE CONTRACTUAL TERMS TO REDUCE RISK IN CLOUD CONTRACTS – GARTNER

based on the fact that the cloud company is prepared to pay more if things go wrong.

Bear in mind too that you may sign up not with the cloud service provider but with a reseller, which could introduce yet another level of complication. You will be signing on the reseller's terms but there could well be a clash with the cloud hosting company – the cloud company could be providing a bronze level of service while the reseller could be offering a gold one.

One way round this is by signing a pass-through contract where the reseller supplies a service from a named supplier such as Amazon or Microsoft.

"Due diligence work needs to be carried out up-front – there is little opportunity for comeback after a problem."

There's no doubt that the market will consolidate over the next few years as the poorer providers are found out and smaller cloud companies will be taken over. While that's happening, look to sign up with an accredited cloud provider, a company that has been endorsed by the Cloud Industry Forum or ISO, for example.

One thing is certain: the due diligence work needs to be carried out up-front – there is little opportunity for comeback after a problem, whether it's a security breach or a service issue. ■

DATA STORAGE IN THE CLOUD - now any firm can benefit

Offsite data backup has long been a staple of enterprise disaster recovery strategies, but it's been too expensive or complex for smaller firms. That's all changed thanks to cloud computing

The benefits are significant...

It doesn't take a genius to work out that multiple copies of your data, stored across disparate servers, is much safer than having all your data eggs in one basket. That can cost a lot of money if it's your own hardware, so look to the cloud where a service provider will be able to duplicate your data across multiple, geographically distributed servers. This significantly cuts the chances of all your data being lost and also brings the same disaster recovery strategies used by large enterprises within reach of much smaller companies.

Complexity costs money, both in terms of infrastructure (such as tape drives, virtual machines, offsite storage and technical staff to maintain it all) and also business downtime (if you have data on tape drives at offsite storage and need to restore servers, the time to recovery becomes stretched). Keeping it simple in the cloud allows smaller organisations to budget for business continuity, with the added value of virtually instant data recovery.

...but watch out for pitfalls

The biggest pitfall of a cloud-based disaster recovery strategy is that you may be at risk with a single supplier. While the ability of the cloud to provide data redundancy across multiple and disparate servers gives a huge amount of confidence, you also have to allow for the worst case scenario: your cloud provider going out of business and taking timely access to your data with it. So to guarantee business continuity, retaining a full backup on your own servers or contracting a secondary cloud service might be wise.

Service level agreements (SLAs) are a vital part of any cloud contract, but they are not a magic bullet that can save your business if things go pear shaped at your cloud storage provider. No matter how contractually watertight your SLA is, if things go wrong all it actually provides is legal leverage. Ensure, therefore, that your SLA explicitly details an agreed remediation process in the event of a failure so that your business does not suffer unduly while waiting for compensation to arrive.

Get the priorities right

Asking the right questions of a cloud storage provider is essential if both the transition to a cloud-based disaster recovery process and its effectiveness once in place are to be trouble free. Proper investigation is vital when it comes to determining if a provider can ▶

"If a cloud provider falls at any of the other due diligence hurdles then it is unsuitable to be trusted with your data."

meet the needs of your business in terms of compliance, security, data handling and recovery.

In fact, the specifics of the data recovery aspects of the service are probably the last things that you should investigate and for good reason: if a cloud provider falls at any of the other due diligence hurdles then it is unsuitable to be trusted with your data.

Remember that cloud-based storage services are still relatively immature, and with companies keen to jump on the bandwagon before the wheels start wobbling it is vital to ensure that any service provider you contract with has an established track record. You will want to know how long they have been trading and how financially stable they are.

It's not that start-up companies are definitely off the radar, but be sure to take into account the impact on your data should a small company be bought out by a larger one that you may have already discounted for whatever reason. So be sure to properly investigate how easy it is to move your data to another provider should you want to terminate your contract at any point.

Security and compliance

If your industry is covered by specific regulatory requirements then your next question must be whether the provider can adhere to them. Obviously, if it cannot, or is unsure, then it's not worth asking any more questions. If it can, then move on to matters of security. Ask obvious questions such as how your data is encrypted, and less obvious ones such as who holds the encryption keys.

Ask about who has access to your data and what controls are in place to prevent both accidental and intentional abuse, but also ask about physical security at the data centres. If your service provider is unable or unwilling to answer your security questions, find one that is.

CLOUD STORAGE – benefits summary

Cloud storage can address many challenges that physical storage doesn't:

- You are not dependent on a single server;
- There is no direct dependency on any hardware;
- You don't have to buy more disk space than you initially need to accommodate future data growth;
- Business continuity is provided in the event of a site disaster;
- A 'virtual' storage container can be provisioned that is larger than the physical space available;
- You can drastically reduce over-provisioning in a pay-as-you-go model;
- You can access your entire storage pool from a single point.

SOURCE: WWW.I365.COM

What about the worst case scenario?

We've already mentioned SLAs, but even though an agreement will not save your data if everything goes wrong, a properly negotiated one could save your business. Ask about business-critical issues such as availability, security and compensation from the start. Deal only with a service provider that is willing to enter into detailed SLA negotiations.

To mitigate any need to resort to the SLA, also ask the provider for full details of its own data protection, recovery and auditing procedures, and don't be afraid to prod them all with your due diligence stick.

What, where and how many?

This is data storage and disaster recovery we are talking about, so be sure to ask appropriate questions of any provider such as how many copies of your data sets are kept, where they are located geographically and how far back your archive stretches. Don't be afraid to get technical and ask about the frequency of data verification tests and availability of verification reports. ■

Who are you? Cloud's problem with identity

Authentication is one of the trickiest obstacles to overcome when it comes to moving to the cloud

ONE OF THE BIGGEST headaches for any business decision maker that has embarked on the move to the cloud is how to secure data and access to it. In fact, cloud is very likely to force the CIO's hand in implementing formal identity and access management policies across their organisation.

Identity management is a relatively mature technology for on-premise infrastructure when compared to what is on offer for any cloud environment.

However, the move to the cloud for most will involve an evolutionary approach. Very few, if any, companies can or will move completely to the cloud, as there are too many legacy systems to maintain that are distinctly cloud-unfriendly. Regulation and compliance will also arrest any movement to a pure cloud environment for enterprises.

Any identity management implementation has to take into account that it will be managing users on legacy systems and those accessing on-premise applications and systems. Those users will want to seamlessly access cloud services, preferably without having to re-present their credentials.

Up until now, identity management has mainly focused on large firms with massive, dedicated IT infrastructures containing numerous users and applications.

CIOs need to consider the expansion of identity management to include other third parties, such as smaller organisations, cloud service providers and government bodies.

Security steps

What steps do CIOs need to take to ensure a successful and secure implementation of identity management in the cloud?

Identity management is just one discipline that CIOs need. There also has to be a complete and robust data model to protect the range of data passing through the cloud, according to Jason Hill, partner at IT consultancy Glue Reply.

"You need to be able to limit what people can see and typically this is done by content-based access (also known as attribute-based assertions), so that you can create a content data field to protect and share information assets," he says.

Hill adds that this approach can be passed along the value chain so that end-to-end collaboration is a possibility. "You can have the best in identity management and content management but you need to limit access appropriately. Remember it's not an application as such but you can lock down you data," he suggests.

Garry Sidaway, global strategy director at IT security provider Integralis, believes that businesses have been

struggling to provide identity services that cover just the internal enterprise let alone the cloud.

"IT has moved from password synchronisation to single sign-on and then provisioning," he says. "Now they are faced with extending this complex issue to the immature cloud."

Sidaway adds that businesses will see more and more cloud service brokers offering identity services to consolidate and manage the issue of providing trusted services to bridge the trust gap between the cloud providers and business.

Covering all bases

Managing provisioning, federation and de-provisioning are also critical when moving your business to the public cloud. Compliance and liability issues will limit how businesses move this trust from the enterprise to the cloud.

"The trust gap will remain until cloud service brokers can ensure continuity and transparency of their services and be able to clearly demonstrate the integrity of these services," Sidaway adds.

The cloud model concentrates on the availability issue of information security, but confidentiality and integrity are critical for businesses thinking of moving to the cloud.

Hill says that he sees identity management being offered more as a service from the cloud.

"There is an identity that is yours as an individual but there is also an identity in terms of authorisation and credentials," he says.

"Accreditation can managed by someone else such as Exostra, the DVLA or HMRC, all of whom can vouch for your credentials meaning that you don't have to keep identity management on premise."

Neil Hollister, chief executive of security company Cryptocard, adds that putting authentication in the cloud automates many of the processes ▶

associated with managing an employee's identity making it easier to spot suspicious activity. Plus if a device is lost, the security profile can be remotely wiped.

"The fact is that as more and more users access data centres, apps and services from ever more varied locations, companies relying on an on-premise model won't be able to keep up," he says. "As a result, vulnerabilities will start to creep in."

"The trust gap will remain until cloud service brokers can ensure continuity and transparency of their services and be able to clearly demonstrate the integrity of these services."

With a SaaS-based model, companies can ensure that they are more effectively managing identity management across the enterprise, while reducing costs.

This is because there is a massive reduction in infrastructure investment in terms of both buying and running. Using authentication-as-a-service, rather than having to host servers and have a dedicated team of people, a small team can manage authentication globally across the business in a way that enables them to scale as new members of staff join and others leave.

FIM

This authentication-as-a-service could lead to firms introducing Federated Identity Management (FIM). This is a process where users are allowed to allocate identity information across security domains dynamically. Recognised authenticated identities can share personalised services across domains. This should increase the portability of digital identities whether they are customers, partners, joint ventures, vendors, affiliates, subsidiaries and employees.

There is no central personal information storage with this method, but users can still link identity information between accounts. Again, significant savings can be made, decreasing costs associated with constant re-provisioning, alleviating security loopholes and resolving the usual user issues caused by inflexible application architecture.

Any organisation with business in the cloud will come across some occasion that entails third party trust. Firms can execute a federated identity model to underwrite against the risk of supporting a business model where there is a strong possibility of third-party risk.

CIOs also need to build a strong business case for the board before implementing any identity management that encompasses on-premise infrastructure and branches out into the cloud. They'll need to show they have cultivated firm measures for negotiating with service providers by concentrating on a few key basics. CIOs will also need to define the dangers of a cloud-based identity management implementation based on regulatory compliance, policies and other requirements.

But it is not just risk that needs to be taken into consideration; trust is an issue important to CIOs and the board when considering the step towards managing identity in the cloud.

"In terms of business this is more about but trust when you look at things like the cloud and business integration you've got to trust your partner," says Hill.

He adds that CIOs need to build a robust model, including what services and functions they provide and what information they provide and consume. "Only then can you then build trust," he concludes. ■

Top five cloud security tips

1 **Encryption equality** – Application encryption on the ground should equal application encryption in the cloud. Firms need to initiate this process by first performing an inventory analysis of all cloud resources to be managed, and then assessing the business risk associated with each element of the IT 'stack'. Appropriate levels of encryption can then be applied.

2 **Mission-critical omissions** – All applications are not the same. So-termed 'extreme' (or high risk) mission-critical cloud-based applications are different, so there will always be some data that you don't host in the cloud. This could be data relating to national security, business intellectual property or sensitive customer account data.

3 **SSL and VPN is the 'ABC'** – Look to see that your cloud provider has basic secure sockets layer (SSL) and virtual private network (VPN) layers in place. This should be among the 'ABC' first principles of cloud security best practice, so that information in transit has a core level of encryption.

4 **Policing policy practice** – Formalised security and access control policies are a prerequisite to using the cloud securely. Whether your firm produces a one-page document or conducts formal in-house training, policy controls are the bedrock of cloud security best practice.

5 **Transparency, clarity and visibility** – Constantly auditing your cloud provider's service for true visibility is crucial. A Ponemon Institute study found that half of all respondents recognise that many cloud resources are not evaluated for security prior to deployment. In practice, the process of pre-evaluation, re-evaluation and audit analysis with a view to achieving application and data transparency, clarity and visibility is essential.

Counting the cost of the cloud

Assessing the cost of moving to cloud is not always about the numbers. Sometimes it's about taking a bit of a gamble

"MANY YEARS AGO, when dinosaurs walked the earth, I was an accountant at British Telecom," recalls Martin Perminas.

Some 25 years later, he is the chief executive of Intelligent SMS specialist Boomerang. Despite such a passage of time, he can still recall one of the biggest hurdles he faced back then.

"When I joined BT, it was at the tipping point of privatisation, and it was full of people who were used to choosing the best engineering solution, regardless of the commercial impact," he says.

"They were very smart people, but they didn't understand why it's important to apply financial criteria to your decisions."

Changing times

Things are very different today. Not just at BT. We are all aware of the need to factor financial considerations into any technology-related decision-making process. That said, it doesn't make things any easier.

"Accounting is not an exact science," says Chas Roy-Chowdhury, head of taxation at the Association of Chartered Certified Accountants.

Although accounting concepts such as return on investment (ROI) and total cost of ownership (TCO) are routinely used to estimate and compare IT costs, there is plenty of room for interpretation.

It's not hard to understand why. Whether you are considering using SaaS, or comparing alternatives such as public clouds vs private clouds, or totting up the bill for maintaining the status quo, there are many cost-related factors to consider. These range from set-up, service and training and overheads such as floor space and electricity, as well as less tangible costs such as those associated with security breaches and diminished performance and their potential impact. Then there are the implications of cloud computing for tax and financial reporting, and the great CapEx OpEx debate.

"It's difficult to work out the cost associated with any technology purchasing decision, but cloud computing is more challenging," Roy-Chowdhury adds, citing barriers such as not being able to compare like with like and not having the benefit of hindsight.

"Being able to access information and infrastructure any time and from anywhere is very advantageous and the short-term benefits of cloud computing may outweigh the long-term cost," he says.

Some cost-related decisions on cloud computing seem to have more to do with gut feeling than hard numbers. "We didn't do any detailed analysis financially, before deciding to run the business in the cloud," claims Gary White, the founder and CEO of White Springs.

Even though the financial analysis was done only 'at a high level' he suggests "the decision was a no-brainer, because the benefits of subscribing to Salesforce.com versus buying and owning the hardware and software were absolutely clear." And they weren't just to do with cost.

Keep focused

White Springs is a fast-growing UK company with operations in Europe and the US, so it was obvious to the CEO that doing it in-house would be a huge effort in terms of resources.

"I wanted my staff to focus on growing the company, not on running the infrastructure," he says. Although White Springs did start out with a PC-based accounting system, as soon as FinancialForce.com was available, it switched to this.

"Gaining greater functionality and better visibility of customer and financial information across the company was ▶

more important than the long-term cost of doing it," he added.

Whilst the benefits of SaaS may loom so large that the long-term financial costs seem irrelevant, things are less straightforward in the world of virtual data centres and Infrastructure as a Service (IaaS). Cloud purists may draw a big line around public clouds and decry private clouds and hybrid clouds as oxymorons, but once these terms entered the marketing-speak of vendors such as Cisco and IBM, cloud computing was redefined. Businesses may as well acknowledge this, and consider the relative costs of all available options.

Ultimately, the decision-making process is not necessarily an 'either, or' choice between a private data centre and an on-demand data centre. In reality, it's a much more complex choice that also includes all sorts of hosted and managed services.

Decisions, decisions

There is also the possibility of combining on-demand public resources with those provided by your own data centre, in what's often described as a 'hybrid cloud'.

The decision of which to opt for may not be as much of a 'no brainer' as choosing SaaS over the on-premise alternative. Although IaaS can provide you with elastic access to computing power, memory, and storage, and charge on a pay-as-you-go basis only for the resources used (without installing new equipment or waiting out the hardware procurement process), there is a downside. One of the big benefits of SaaS is its capacity to relieve the user of all of the burdens associated with software maintenance and upgrades; IaaS requires a little more attention.

Somebody has to monitor, manage, and patch your on-demand infrastructure. There are software tools designed specifically to help you do all of this, but while some organisations are comfortable doing this themselves, others prefer to hand it over to a third party. That's one of the reasons a variety of hosted, managed service and outsourced solutions are being labelled and marketed as private clouds, and one of the reasons why there are so many possible approaches to financing.

For example, in a private cloud where you pay for the software licences and own the boxes, there are various ways to avoid taking the hit up front. Financing options include contract hire, hire purchase, loans, and various types of lease. A private cloud can't exploit the buying power of the public cloud, so the relative costs may be higher, and, unless you invest in some very big boxes, you aren't going to have the elasticity of the public cloud (though you may think you're never going to need it), but you can exploit virtualisation to better use the computing resources you do have in your private cloud.

"After a series of acquisitions we had three operating divisions at 25 locations

and a hotchpotch of systems," explains Ian Johnson, chief financial officer at Asbestos removal and management contractor Silverdell.

"When we reviewed the IT infrastructure and support we quickly realised we weren't big enough to support our own internal IT team," he says. The firm decided that "a private cloud and virtual desktops were the most cost effective solution."

"It's difficult to work out the cost associated with any technology purchasing decision, but cloud computing is more challenging."

Johnson adds: "For what one competent IT head would have cost us, we were able to get a hosted solution."

This provides web-based access to processing power and applications, and the desktops have been virtualised for the operating divisions – also using the most cost-effective solution.

"We considered Citrix and Microsoft desktop virtualisation, but 2X offered the best price-performance ratio," adds John Abrahams, technical director at IT Managed Services, which looks after Silverdell's software licences, infrastructure maintenance and staff support, in an arrangement backed up by a personalised Service Level Agreement (SLA).

Devil's in the detail

Some words of caution: If you don't factor the terms of your SLA into your cost benefit analyses, you could end up paying for services you can't use, or have no intention of using.

This is what happened to one software engineer who didn't read his Amazon Web Services contract well enough to know what he would be billed for, when the meter would be running, and when it would stop running.

"I put some test virtual machines on the servers of AWS, and for a while my bills were just a few pennies each, so when I got a monthly bill for $40 I was a bit surprised," said Adam Ramsay. "Turns out, when I finished the tests, I forgot to turn off the Virtual Private Network." ■

Financial benefits of cloud computing and services

Factor	On-premise	Cloud computing
Expenditure type	Capital expenditure (capex) Operating expense (opex)	Operating expense (opex)
Cash flow	Servers and software are purchased upfront	Payments are made as the service is provided
Financial risk	Entire financial risk is taken upfront, with uncertain return	Financial risk is taken monthly and is matched to return
Income statement	Maintenance and depreciated capital expense	Maintenance expense only
Balance sheet	Software and hardware are carried as a long-term capital asset	Nothing appears on the balance sheet

SOURCE: TALKING TO YOUR CFO ABOUT CLOUD COMPUTING, FORRESTER RESEARCH

The Cloud: a business accelerator?

Don't let your IT infrastructure dictate the pace of your company's growth.

Over the past few years no concept in the world of computer technology has generated more buzz than Cloud Computing. According to some it is the next generation of hosting solutions, a new way of thinking the relationship between corporations and their IT infrastructure. But what is Cloud Computing exactly?

Imagine hundreds of thousands of servers clustered in different locations worldwide and linked by a common network, the Internet, allowing for unprecedented economies of scale. As such, Cloud Computing comes as a service: resources, available immediately and billed according to usage. IT is no longer a cost centre for a company, it's a commodity: Welcome to the "cloud"!

In the era of web 2.0, social media tidal waves can appear and disappear in the blink of an eye. Where will the next one occur and how can a company be prepared for the exponential traffic and power requirement associated with it? Cloud Computing is the solution, offering the possibility to rapidly add resources:CPU, RAM and storage, and allowing your infrastructure to evolve temporarily to meet the challenge. Flexibility and scalability are certainly one of the most significant benefits of the Cloud. An entire infrastructure can be available, virtually, in a matter of minutes and new projects launched in a matter of seconds, when it used to take months to build an infrastructure.

The absence of physical infrastructures is also synonymous with lower costs. A company no longer needs to invest large amounts of money to build a datacentre. It can rent it. In this way, Cloud Computing also eliminates structural overallocation. A company only pays for the resources it uses and returns them once they are no longer needed.

Konbini, a French Web TV Service gets more than 150 000 visits a day and broadcasts about 10 Million videos each month. At the forefront of web 2.0, the company moved its infrastructure into the Cloud in the first half of 2011. Results were spectacular: IT expenses divided by 3, the ability to scale up and down its hosting power with a single click and the possibility to focus on its core activity resulting in the creation of a new time-shifting feature.

This is perhaps the best example of the Cloud's full potential. From being a simple tool used to cut costs and simplify corporate IT, Cloud Computing is gradually turning into a project accelerator and radically changing the way companies approach their line of business. This ship hasn't sailed yet... but you might want to get on board very soon.

To find the best solution for your business, contact us on 020 7357 6616 or visit our website www.ovh.co.uk

Entrust it to the European leader

When switching to Cloud Computing, the choice of an IT operator plays a crucial role in the process, and the company you choose must offer the highest guarantees in terms of reliability, performance and security. This choice is especially important as a successful transition to the Cloud depends on the quality of the provider's network, both in terms of bandwidth and equipment.

OVH, the European leader on the web-hosting market and the world's fourth largest web-hosting company* is uniquely positioned to assist companies with their course leading to the Cloud. Since 1999 OVH has deployed its own fibre optic network across Europe: a unique infrastructure on the market. Its characteristics are staggering: a 1000 Gbps bandwidth, a lossless connection over 31 peering points in 3 different continents as well as 24/7 operational maintenance. This network is also fully redundant.

As of 2010, OVH has invested more than £8.9 million to build a Cloud-ready infrastructure. This was materialized by the construction of Tier IV data centres (the highest certification level in the world) and the duplication of all resources (each server, storage space and network access is doubled to guarantee service continuity). However, these investments have no impact on costs with prices among the lowest on the market.

The Private Cloud solution made in OVH

- Quick project implementation: deploy a ready for use infrastructure in a few minutes.
- Dynamic management: with Private Cloud, companies can take advantage of a scalable and flexible infrastructure. If a peak load occurs, they can allocate more resources to their project with a few simple clicks.
- Fully integrated security: protect yourself from all types of risks by combining a fully redundant infrastructure with VMware© solutions.
- Secure exchanges: every Private Cloud infrastructure is dedicated to a single customer. And with private networks (VLAN), access is restricted to only the customer.
- Business continuity: OVH guarantees its customers 100% availability of its Cloud services. Everything is set up so that users do not have to suffer from service interruption: equipment, network and electricity supply are fully redundant.
- A single management interface: find all the VMware© features you need, manage all your resources from your vSphere or vCloud interface.

Packaged solutions to get a head start

OVH offers several starting packages which include all the resources necessary to start out immediately: servers, storage space, network access as well as VMware© licenses. And during the ordering process, companies can immediately add servers, storage space or IP blocks. A few minutes later, their datacentre is ready to host all of their applications!

Free Test FOR 15 DAYS
FOR 2 HOSTS
ONE 300 GB HOST
LIMITED INTERNET CONNECTION
no obligation

To test this offer, use promo code PCCUK
For more information, visit our website www.ovh.co.uk/PC
or call us at 020 7357 6616

*Source: Netcraft January 2012

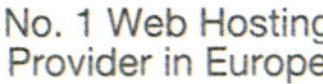

Is the cloud green?

Is cloud computing a greener way to go with IT? Supporters would argue yes, but it's a complex calculation to prove it in detail

SOMETHING STRANGE HAS happened in the last decade: green issues – which used to be the preserve of hippies and environmentalists – have quietly invaded the mainstream. One can scarcely look at a new service for anything these days without being reminded of its green credentials. New car? Fewer emissions. New boiler? Energy efficient. New light bulb? Eco-friendly.

Needless to say, this philosophy has permeated the IT industry too, with much more attention being paid to the energy rating of servers and PCs than there has been in previous years.

Cloud computing has been a key part of this debate and there's a long-running discussion on whether the technology is energy efficient or not. So how does a company interested in maintaining its green credentials go about deciding whether to go down the cloud route or not? After all, you may need to show what your IT is consuming as part of a statutory carbon audit, especially in larger companies. Regulation on energy use can only increase in the future.

> **"A move to the cloud in the US would deliver CO_2 reductions of 85.7m tonnes each year, the equivalent of nearly 200 million barrels of oil."**

It's not an easy question to answer. On one hand, we have a school of thought that says because cloud computing data centres are not adding to the actual computing power, but are using servers more efficiently, then they are, by definition, the greener option. There are opponents, however, who say that there are some big questions to be answered first and that the blanket statement that cloud computing is greener is a misleading one. It's getting to be a heated debate – with both sides brandishing the figures to support their case.

The latest entrant in this form of climate war is research company, Verdantix, which released a report in 2011 claiming that American companies could drastically cut CO_2 emissions by turning to cloud computing. According to the report, a wholesale move to cloud delivery would deliver CO_2 emission reductions of 85.7m tonnes each year, the equivalent of nearly 200 million barrels of oil.

That translates into energy savings for US businesses of $12.3 billion in the next 10 years if they adopt cloud services. The Verdantix research predicts that the financial benefits from energy reduction and increased IT efficiency in 2011 alone would reach $824 million by the end of the year in the US.

Meanwhile Pike Research has

predicted that cloud computing will lead to a 38 per cent reduction in worldwide data centre energy expenditures by 2020. Microsoft too has said that the cloud can cut energy consumption and carbon emissions by 30 per cent or more.

In May 2012, fellow tech giant Apple announced plans to power its iCloud data centre with green energy while, elsewhere, computer makers are busy making components such as memory and processors more efficient too.

The Verdantix survey was sponsored by the Carbon Disclosure Project – an organisation with a vested interest in promoting green measures. And it wasn't long before dissenters were rounding on the research findings and finding flaws in the argument.

What's the energy source?

One of the main critics of the survey, GreenMonk analyst Tom Raftery, pointed out that there had been some rather dubious assumptions. "The mistake here is presuming a direct relationship between energy and carbon emissions. While this might seem like a logical assumption, it is not necessarily valid," he wrote.

"If I have a company whose energy retailer is selling me power generated primarily by nuclear or renewable sources for example, and I move my ▶

applications to a cloud provider whose power comes mostly from coal, then the move to cloud computing will increase, not decrease, my carbon emissions."

This is the key to many of the arguments: what is the source of the power that is driving those data centres? It was a question raised by Greenpeace in 2010 when it published a report, 'How dirty is your data?', pointing out that there were serious concerns about some of the big players in cloud computing.

Gary Cook, the lead author of that report, said that the problem was the lack of transparency from some of the cloud companies. He agreed, however, that data centre and server design innovation can greatly improve efficiency and reduce overheads in energy demand. He said that more in the sector were comfortable with sharing best-practice data, but that without more transparency, such efforts were not worth much.

Cook has a point and some cloud providers have indeed been rather secretive about their operations, and to try to get an idea of how energy efficient their servers are would prove to be impossible. But data centre specialists themselves – those that host many clients – are currently vying with each other for the accolade of running the world's greenest facilities, with all sorts of design and supply innovations in the way they are built, located and fuelled.

The problem is that even with an overall rating for the efficiency of data centres, the actual usage of a set of servers by a client is much more difficult to assess, and detailed breakdown of the rating by factors such as the energy type can make comparisons less valid.

"The Green Grid has developed a model that has clear goals for improving energy efficiency."

Location, location...

A good case in point has been an argument made by Greenpeace about a data centre run by Facebook in Oregon, which takes much of its power from coal-fired sources. But, in fact, it is said to be one of the world's more efficient facilities, because the cool climate in the state allows it to run without mechanical chillers, one the biggest energy hogs in a data centre.

One organisation that is trying to improve the way in which sustainable computing is reported is the Green Grid, a non-profit consortium of end-users, policy makers, technology providers, facility architects and utility companies looking to improve the efficiency of data centres.

Ali Moinuddin at data centre player, Interxion, is also the European communications committee co-chair of the Green Grid and is aware that there needs to be a better standard of assessment. "The green data centre is at the heart of the whole movement towards sustainable computing. We need to move beyond just considering power

Who's the greenest of them all?

The ultimate in green data centres could be Icelandic cloud provider, GreenQloud, which uses geothermal energy to power its data centre, with a lot of hydroelectric power thrown in for good measure.

Of course, there aren't many cloud providers that are sitting in a geographic region with millions of litres of naturally heated water on tap. The company uses 100% renewable energy drawn from the Icelandic grid, which is 30% geothermal and 70% hydro.

CEO Eirikur Hrafnsson says that data centres that claim to be green base the claim on spurious reasoning. "When big players talk about their 'greenness' all they are saying is that their data centres are now more efficient in cooling IT equipment. Energy efficiency of data centres and servers cannot keep up with future energy needs and be effective in reducing carbon dioxide emissions. We need to change the energy sources to renewables; it's that simple."

And in a lesson to other providers, the company records all energy use and carbon emissions made by each customer and makes the data freely available to them.

There are certainly other providers that would claim equal credentials with GreenQloud. In the UK, Capgemini's Merlin data centre, in Swindon, is said to be setting a global standard for energy efficiency, with a power usage effectiveness (PUE) rating of just 1.08 (1 would be perfect). Next Generation Data (NGD) Europe, based in Newport, Wales, is claiming to be the first in Europe to run on 100% renewable energy. And Telehouse takes waste heat from a centre in London's East End to pipe hot water to 1,000 local homes, free of charge.

usage effectiveness [PUE – a standard metric for data centres], to carbon usage effectiveness (CUE) and water usage effectiveness (WUE)," he says (water is often used for cooling).

"It makes environmental and business sense to evaluate these metrics. The Green Grid has developed the Data Center Maturity Model that sets goals for improving energy efficiency and sustainability across all aspects of the data centre."

Meanwhile, there are a range of questions for a company interested in cloud and green issues to ask a provider:

- What's the energy source of the data centre?
- What metrics does it use to measure energy efficiency?
- What measures has it taken to reduce power consumption?
- What temperature does it run its data centre at?
- If the cloud provider describes itself as green, what criteria has it deployed (planting a few trees outside isn't going to cut it)?
- What information does it provide to its own customers when it comes to energy consumption?

Energy consumption has really only been debated for a few years now, so it's not surprising that there's confusion around.

Regardless of this, it is not an issue that's going to go away. Far from it. Indeed, many companies - large and small - are interested in energy saving measures so cloud computing providers, whether they like it or not, are just going to have to get used to the idea of being more open. ■

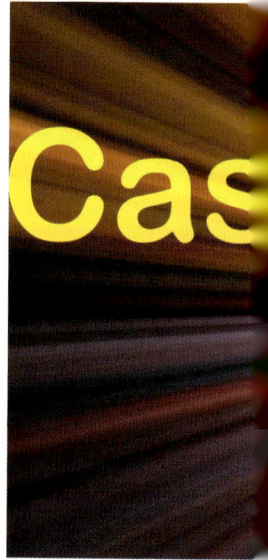

CASE STUDIES: Words from the wise

Every business is different, as is every cloud computing implementation. That said, we can still benefit from the experience of others. Read on for a selection of real-world cloud case studies

IF YOU'VE READ THIS FAR, you'll be armed with hints and tips from the experts about what cloud computing is and how it can help you and your business. But the best is yet to come. There is no greater expert advice than from those who've already been there, done that, bought the T-shirt and come out the other side.

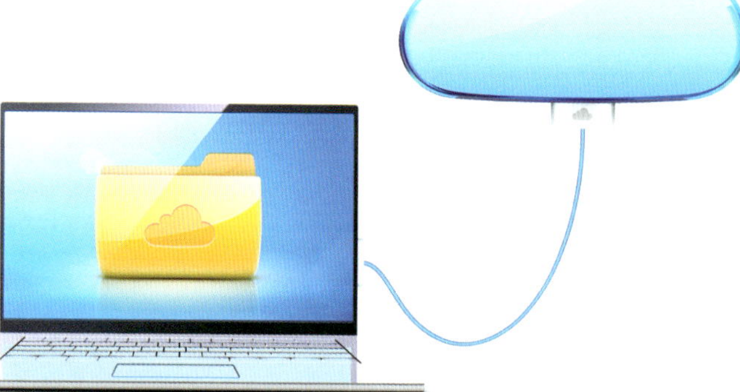

More business applications in the cloud

- Human resources (HR) systems are not obvious targets for the cloud but vendors such as SuccessFactors are proving that properly managing the entire workforce in terms of skills, knowledge and structure can have a big impact on business performance. European users such as construction supplier Hilti are big fans.

- The public sector has much to gain from the cloud – in the NHS, County Durham and Darlington Foundation Trust, a consortium of 10 organisations, is using Wax Digital's web3 procurement system to make it easier for staff across the consortium to select goods and services for purchase and place orders quickly and simply, enabling streamlined financial control and authorisation, and accelerating the supply process to nearly always 'next day'.

- Project management is a shoo-in for the cloud, as Vodafone is discovering with the Projectplace web-based communication systems. "Finally we have a central system for storing files, working on them and retrieving them, always in real-time. Any project member can access it, and most importantly, the latest version is always available," says Alexander Gottschlich, global programme manager at Vodafone.

- The Green House, a small Northampton-based business specialising in environmental services, manages around 500,000 scheduled collections a year through its recycling division alone. In the past, all of these transactions would have been carried out manually. Issues were typically sorted out over the telephone with multiple calls routinely taking place between the company, its suppliers and clients. This was a time-consuming, resource-intensive and expensive process. Today, the company manages all of these collections through Salesforce.com's Service Cloud, into which it has integrated a large number of workflows and approval procedures.

Channel 4

The TV giant looked to the cloud to help it handle the 'Davina effect'

Company profile

Channel 4 went live in November 1982, with the first programme aired being Countdown. Since then, what was originally one channel has grown into a firm spanning a number of channels including Film4 and E4, on demand services, a website and more. The firm is not beholden to shareholders and therefore generates the majority of its funding through advertising and sponsorship.

IN SOME WAYS, perhaps it was inevitable Channel 4 would be one of the pace-setters when it came to cloud computing. After all, the television channel earned its reputation for a host of innovative programmes, so the company's decision to become an early adopter of Amazon cloud services could be regarded as the perfect marriage.

And, yet, the move to Amazon came about almost by accident. In what sounds like a technological version of those footballing stories where a scout tries to sign a promising schoolboy and comes back with another player, the broadcaster first started investigating another product altogether.

"One of our guys went to a conference and learned about Amazon's S3 product," says Bob Harris, Channel 4's CTO. "But when we looked into it, it was clear that it wasn't S3 that we wanted but EC2".

Back then, Channel 4 was trying to streamline its web hosting. The company had a variety of sites, all supporting individual TV programmes, but it wanted a more concerted approach and greater scalability.

A cloud-based solution was the obvious answer so the company started to look around for a supplier. At the time, the clear market leader was Amazon, but Channel 4 also examined alternative providers and concentrated on some UK ones to simplify concerns about physical location of data. The results were not satisfactory, according to Harris. "One provider actually asked us to 'back-off' as they felt we might overwhelm their service," he says.

The clear choice then was Amazon, but it wasn't purely because it was the market leader and had the economic clout. There were several other factors too, according to Harris.

"Even back then AWS was already displaying the traits which are a must for a credible public cloud provider: self-provisioning, pay as you go pricing, and elasticity," he says. "Since then, AWS has evolved adding new features and services, at both the IaaS and PaaS levels, which make it relatively straightforward to build complex platforms quickly and turn them off again when no longer required."

By the nature of its

"We spent time talking to Amazon about its approach to security and made sure we kept security high on our agenda at all times."

business, Channel 4 expects a lot of peaks for its web efforts. The website for a popular TV programme, for example, could potentially expect hundreds and thousands of visitors over a short period of time. Luckily, the Amazon-supported sites have handled everything that has been thrown that way.

From small beginnings, Channel 4 has quickly moved towards cloud being the default platform for all websites within the organisation. Harris wouldn't say exactly how many are supported, but he would say there were more than 50 sites.

Part of the appeal of cloud is the fluidity and the ability to put up (and take down) sites quickly and Channel 4 certainly makes the most of this.

"Being a TV channel, we have the ability to drive huge peaks of traffic to sites when somebody on air says "go to www.xx.com now" – I call it the 'Davina factor'. The ability to scale those sites to meet those peaks is something I really wish I'd had back in the early 2000s when we started running Big Brother," Harris adds.

It wasn't all plain sailing though. There were plenty of concerns about moving to cloud, notably the security implications, and Harris had to make sure those worries were dealt with.

"We spent time talking to Amazon about its approach to security and made sure we kept security high on our agenda at all times. Amazon's security credentials are pretty impressive (ISO27001, SAS70, PCI(L1), HIPPA) and before going to another public cloud provider I'd want to be sure they place the same focus on security as Amazon does," he says.

One of the other key advantages that Amazon had was its reliability. However, Harris was not a big fan of SLAs: "I'm not interested in getting money back," he says. "I want a provider that knows what it's doing and can provide a proper service."

Harris did admit there was a psychological mindset to overcome, but said that by picking advocates for cloud computing it is possible to convert some of the sceptics.

Channel 4 is certainly committed to the cloud approach and hasn't looked beyond Amazon thus far, but the firm hasn't ruled out doing so in the future.

"As the importance of cloud with Channel 4 grows, we will take a step back and, at least, reappraise the wider market as several, potentially credible, players have entered this space in the last couple of years," he says.

The reliability and scalability of the service has laid down a marker for other companies to beat. Indeed, the sheer number of websites continuing to run, despite the attentions of a peak TV audience is a compelling argument and ensures that Channel 4 is a prime example of how cloud computing can meet the most stringent demands. ■

Lush

Thanks to cloud computing, the ethical cosmetics company can now collate data and report on its environmental impact

Company profile

Lush is a successful UK handmade cosmetics company headquartered in Poole. Known for its campaigning efforts on environmental issues and reducing its environmental impact in product design, manufacturing and selling, it is also against animal testing and the use of animal fats in its products. It has built its privately owned business of 102 UK stores and an online shopping website over 17 years maintaining this strong ethical stance.

LUSH'S ETHICAL STANCE lies at the core of everything it does. These efforts start with the sourcing of ethical suppliers of raw materials that do not use animal products or those tested on animals.

Palm oil is another product the company is looking to remove from its manufacturing process completely while the use of cocoa butter is currently under review, says Ruth Andrade, Lush's environmental officer.

"Then there are the products, which go on up the supply chain, and all the waste produced and energy consumed in our factories and stores," she says.

"As both a manufacturer and retailer we are privileged to be allowed to try new things, like starting our own sustainable oil project or promoting local organic agriculture."

All of these operations and initiatives need to be monitored somehow, which is why the company recently started to use CloudApps software.

"We measure 100 indicators across over 100 stores," Andrade explained. "We were getting into having thousands of spreadsheets, but this was a highly manual and painful process. We can now collate all of this data through CloudApps as a single source."

CloudApps' Sustainability Suite captures and discloses the company's 'environmental footprint,' which includes measurements on water and energy use, travel, waste generation and packaging across all of Lush's 102 stores, eight main offices and eight factory sites in the UK.

The company only signed up for the software in early 2012, so it has yet to fully realise all of the benefits on offer. That said, Andrade believes the very fact that CloudApps will centralise all of the data Lush generates in relation to sustainability will help it not only optimise the efficiency of its manufacturing, supply chain and retail operations, but also aid in the day-to-day running of the business.

"We liked the fact that the information be accessed from anywhere with a secure internet connection."

"Having a central place to collect data, reports and analysis that compares one indicator to another means we can track indicators like our store energy use per square metre," she says.

"It also means our store dashboards contain the name of the manager, the annual rent, utility bill and everything else I need to know about each shop."

The company plans to use the central system's collaborative functionality to increase staff communication and project management capabilities.

"I can also see if a store is having a problem with maintenance, waste, the air conditioning and even what kind of air curtain it uses," Andrade adds. "It is providing us with an area where we can log calls, put in comments and generally improve our day-to-day collaboration and management."

The fact that CloudApps uses a cloud-based delivery model was a definite advantage for Lush, as the company's counterparts in the US and Japan are existing users of the technology.

"We liked the fact that the information be accessed from anywhere with a secure internet connection," Andrade continues. "We accept that CloudApps will always be more efficient at running its own systems in the cloud than we ever could. What we need to look into now is how efficiently the Salesforce.com data centres that host CloudApps are powered."

Having opted to configure the software themselves after receiving training from CloudApps, Andrade and a group colleagues are in the process of setting up fields, importing data and customising it to the Lush's particular requirements.

She reported that the full transfer of initial data, including utility and store smart meter network information, was not yet complete, but that once it was the company was planning to use CloudApps to generate more in-depth reports and benchmarks that would ultimately help guide it to run the business more ethically and efficiently.

"It will be good to see how things like water usage in-store relates directly to sales, which we use in demonstrating our products, for example," Andrade says.

This capability will, in turn, enable better comparison of performance between sites in support of "more concrete goals," according to Andrade.

"There is also the potential for using its project management features. But for now, it will be mainly used for reporting on the central initiatives in the cloud we already had in place," she adds.

Having such cloud computing resources is also an advantage for Lush when it comes to running the databases behind its freight reports and health and safety data.

"If the team are still using it in a year's time, then we will know it works. If they think it's worth the time inputting the data because the view it gives them of the business helps them run it better than it will be helping to improve the business," Andrade says.

"At Lush, we know there is always more to do. With CloudApps' solution we are to accurately measure, analyse and report our total operational impact in real time. It allows us to accurately manage the sustainability goals we have signed up to, for the benefit of the environment we live in and to reduce our operational costs." ■

Mitchells & Butlers

The pub chain has called last orders on its network and embraced cloud computing

Company profile

Established in 1898, Mitchells & Butlers is a leading operator of some 1,600 restaurants and pubs in the UK, employing around 40,000 staff. Its portfolio of 13 brands includes Harvester, Toby Carvery, Vintage Inns, Premium Country Dining Group, Crown Carveries, Sizzling Pubs, Browns, Miller & Carter, Metro Professionals, All Bar One, Nicholson's, O'Neill's and Ember Inns. Each year the company's brands serve a combined total of 435 million and 125 million drinks and meals respectively.

LIKE MANY ORGANISATIONS Mitchells & Butlers has become increasingly reliant on not only IT systems at its offices to manage its business, but also internal and customer-facing systems in its outlets. The network connectivity for all of these sites is therefore crucial. However, the firm's legacy networking resource was ageing.

The company started looking for an IT supplier with the power to provide its outlets, offices and, ultimately, customers with fast and efficient access to network-based IT services and applications, according to CIO Tony Bentham.

"We are a very large company, with over 1,600 outlets. We also acquire and sell outlets very often. So we buy in almost all of our IT services – the network included," he says.

"We needed a service that was dynamic. Flexibility was key for us, as was taking on a service that would deliver flexibility for our cost base as well."

As part of the transformation of its core IT infrastructure Mitchells & Butlers put its network requirements for the roll out of hosted IT network provision across its entire estate out to tender.

Every response included a cloud-based proposal, according to Bentham. "It's a sign of the times and where everyone is headed," he comments. "Right now, we're very much still in the private cloud, but I believe hybrid cloud models will become more popular in future."

In the end, the company decided to refresh its network with existing IT supplier Fujitsu. Bentham said the company had already provided connectivity between its data centres and some of its outlets. The deal was completed at the end of 2011 and the handover to the hosted cloud-based network services of Fujitsu was completed four months later.

The end-to-end managed network offering connects the firm's offices, restaurants and pubs to applications and services delivered from the cloud. This includes digital

"We needed a service that was dynamic. Flexibility was key for us, as was taking on a service that would deliver flexibility for our cost base as well."

subscriber line (DSL) based Wide Area Network (WAN) services as well as Ethernet for offices. The consumption-based services also include wired and wireless Local Area Network (LAN) connectivity to support individual outlet needs, from access to central applications and services to the point-of-sale terminals (POS) to take payments.

Mitchells & Butlers worked closely with Fujitsu to implement an agile IT infrastructure that underpins its expansion and growth plans. The hosted network solution was designed to improve both how and what its growing UK network of restaurants and pubs access through the network, according to Bentham.

"Our previous solution had been in place for well over a decade and so this service is part of the basic transformation of the ageing parts of our IT infrastructure," he adds. "So, when we looked at Fujitsu's data centres we were satisfied there was sufficient capacity to support future growth."

The roll out was also achieved with minimum disruption and zero downtime. The hosted network lays the foundation for initiatives such as guest Wi-Fi and the deployment of advanced ordering and payment systems using both in-house and guests' own mobile technology.

The network transition is enabling Mitchells & Butlers to provide guests and employees with enhanced services and supports the group's growth plans by improving operational agility and end-user experience.

"It exceeds expectations in terms of reliability and performance," Bentham says. "Migration was smooth, considering the scale of our estate."

And, while he did not share exact figures, Bentham said the cost savings have been considerable.

One of benefits of the new cloud-based network is it removes bandwidth worries, according to Bentham. "This is important, as we use a lot of IT and media-based systems in our outlets, including lots of customer-facing technology," he says, adding that the ability to deliver agility across such a disparate range of outlets, in addition to provide advanced systems, lies entirely in the network.

The new network capability also supports a recent deal the company signed to update its customer Wi-Fi offering. This deal will see O2 Wi-Fi hotspots roll out to all Mitchells & Butlers' outlets, offering guests access to free Wi-Fi. The first hotspots are initially being deployed to 199 Harvester restaurants, while the rollout to the remaining restaurants and pubs will be completed towards the end 2012.

Going forward, Bentham says the two companies will work together to fine tune service levels. "The relationship is very much outcome based. We rely on it to provide a fully resilient, scalable network. And, since the migration, we've had no degradation of performance at all," he says. "We've also noticed that applications are running on average 10 per cent faster and those reliant on databases 30 per cent faster compared with our old network."

Bentham concludes: "Fujitsu is providing us with a network platform for future growth that, with server virtualisation, will save the company further costs and enhance the network end-user experience." ■

Netflix

The online film giant has tested and stretched the cloud's capabilities

Company profile

Netflix is a web-based subscription company that allows users to rent films and TV programmes. It was founded in 1997 and, in addition to employing some 900 people, now boasts more than 25 million streaming members. Available in the US for some time, the service launched in the UK and Ireland in 2012.

NETFLIX IS A CLASSIC example of the way that cloud services have the power to transform a business.

Originally a DVD-by-post business, which boasted 10 to 15 million subscribers, Netflix moved towards the cloud in the last three years to support its growing online streaming services. In December of 2011, Netflix reported that it had 23 million streaming users in the US and Canada and made a push into the UK and Irish markets in January 2012, with a view to the wider European market.

Netflix's cloud architect Adrian Cockcroft is the man behind the technology.

"In 2008 and 2009, we decided to go for the cloud to see if that would support the streaming business, because it was growing unpredictably and fast," Cockcroft explains. This led to Netflix's first dalliance with the cloud and the beginnings of a well-established relationship with Amazon Web Services (AWS).

"During 2010 we had a forced run for the cloud where we knew by the end of the year that we would not be able to run Netflix in our data centres. So we had to get launched in the cloud by the end of the year and during the summer of 2010 we got most of the stuff out there," he adds.

The key to Netflix's cloud venture is the open source database management system Apache Cassandra and AWS. When combined they allow Netflix to extend its services into a whole host of new territories, supporting infinite numbers of users and offering the agility, flexibility and cost effectiveness to scale that an operation the size of Netflix needs to conquer the globe.

"The entire Cassandra structure costs a fraction and can be deployed in seconds," says Cockcroft.

As Netflix spreads into new territories, it's clear that the number of Cassandra clusters it runs will grow significantly. Cockcroft has already been preparing for this expansion, testing the limits of AWS and scaling when necessary. The Cassandra cluster is between six and 24 instances, with a benchmark of 288.

"We're running a multi-billion dollar business with a growth rate that's comparable to that of a tiny start-up. So us being wrong isn't add two machines, it's add three hundred machines and it's

"We can look at ten thousand movies, pick the right ones, and sort them for you in half a second in memory on a Java machine."

very hard to do that in a data centre. So we leverage the cloud to do that," Cockcroft adds.

He sums up the architecture of the Netflix system as "primarily built on AWS, written in Java and then we've got an enterprise scale, globally distributed Platform-as-a-Service that we've build internally. There are Tomcat servers, lots of Java code and big fat machines running."

Using the Red Hat-based CentOS Linux distribution, with a platform programmed entirely in Java, the sheer scale and complexity of the systems and services Netflix uses in the cloud to support its millions of users is difficult to comprehend.

"We've been using Java for many years at Netflix," Cockcroft says.

"We're running heavy duty, number crunching personalisation algorithms. We're caching Gigabytes of data in order to generate this set of a thousand or so movies that we recommend when you start up the Netflix user interface. We can look at ten thousand movies, pick the right ones, and sort them for you in half a second in memory on a Java machine."

The multi-billion dollar business has an engineering team to match. Cockroft calls it "a fairly large team of engineers; a few hundred engineers all individually creating their own little service that runs in the cloud and every service calls everyone else, so it's a big chatty mess."

Netflix shows all the signs of being a global operation. Its headquarters and old data centre are based in San Francisco, but its code runs on Amazon servers in Ireland and the east and west of the US - although it also has a data centre in Singapore. In 2011, Amazon opened two new data centres, in Japan and Brazil, in anticipation of Netflix's venturing in the South American market.

Cockcroft is confident that "as Netflix grows across the world Amazon has the infrastructure to support it globally."

Recently, Netflix started open-sourcing large chunks of its code base. In February 2012, Netflix announced on its tech blog the open-sourcing of Priam, a new management tool that runs alongside Cassandra. Released under the Apache licence, the tool backs up data centres on the fly and works on configuration and token management. It follows the earlier open-sourcing of Astyanax, a replacement Cassandra client, written in Java which allows low level access to Cassandra Remote Procedure Calls (RPC).

Since the release of Cassandra, open-source projects have taken a classical theme, with names straight out of the pages of the Iliad. Not content with Cassandra, the Trojan male line Priam, Hector and Astyanax have also featured. There is a strange juxtaposition between the battlements of Troy and the trenches of big data.

As yet there are no figures to tell us how Netflix's incursion into the UK and Irish markets are going, but Cockcroft hints it has been better than expected.

Only time will tell if Netflix has really managed to capture the hearts, minds and wallets of the British public. But the company is already well aware that cloud services can support its growth. ■

Richmond Events

Cloud hosting from Star has helped the firm 'change the face of events in the UK'

Company profile

Founded in 1989, Richmond Events provides conferences in the UK in a bold new format based on personalised meeting agendas and one-to-one supplier meetings. These are all contained within multi-day events which are free-to-attend for delegates and targeted at specific job roles.

FROM ITS ROOTS over 20 years ago, Richmond Events' business model has relied on advanced database marketing – even before such a term was commonplace. The 75-employee, London-based business still relies heavily on the intellectual property contained within its global IT systems to stay ahead of fierce competition from rivals.

However, as the business evolved, the firm needed more flexible IT to deal with the growing data of conference schedules and the increasing complexity.

"Our uniqueness is that delegates attending our events can create individual itineraries and no two itineraries are the same," says Liam Quinn, IT director at Richmond Events.

"People may not realise how complex a task this is, but it means all of our websites and CRM systems are bespoke. Customers can select from a richer set of supplier and conference information and in turn disclose more preferences."

As an early adopter of managed hosted services from Star, the flexibility offered has been a lifesaver for the company. While customer expectations have grown, the number of employees available to service these needs has gone the other way. Add to that the bubble bursting in 2000 and 11 September 2001, a significant downturn meant the company needed to re-size to survive.

Fortunately, the absence of substantial and inflexible investments in servers, software licences and the use of standardised, virtual desktops (rather than PCs) meant IT could make the right business decision and scale down to a workforce around 50 per cent of its pre-downturn level, without reducing operational capability.

"Just because we use a managed service provider doesn't mean we don't have control. We require the flexibility to run our business how we want to, yet have the support we need."

The subsequent procurement process was changed forever, keeping the cloud essentials of flexibility, agility and option to scale up as well as down whenever required, as top priorities.

This did lead to a change in the role of IT though, with a team not needed for keeping the lights on but ensuring the customer experience was top notch.

This means employees get a much

richer service and Quinn can focus his resources on the core business, maintaining the company's differentiation in the events market it operates in.

"Thanks to our eight years of experience with managed services, our day-to-day activities have changed significantly," he says.

"We are no longer engaged in the typical cycle of daily interventions an IT team has to make just to keep the systems and people working. For a business of our size this would be a terrible drain on resources."

Quinn adds: "Now, we are free to focus on areas like the support model - not necessarily what the escalation processes look like on paper - more how it works in real life."

Moving to cloud services though does not mean a life of leisure for Quinn's team. Rather there is a greater focus on the service levels that the business requires.

"Just because we use a managed service provider doesn't mean we don't have control. We require the flexibility to run our business how we want to, yet have the support we need," he says.

"Our customer teams are in constant communication to clients and potential clients all day and we must make sure they have access to the tools they need to facilitate the sales which are the lifeblood of our operations and must happen very smoothly."

Quinn claimed to have chosen Star for both its technical ability and its "credible reputation," something he saw as key for any cloud implementation.

"Over the years I have found that selecting partners with a similar culture and positive attitude towards doing business with you is always reflected in the quality of service you get," he says.

"As an IT buyer our custom has to be important to the partners we choose if we are to get good value. I never want to be a big fish in a small pond, or worse still, a small fish in a big pond."

Looking back on Richmond Events' experience, it is clear that a similar path will be followed by many UK companies, who are just embarking on their cloud journey. Whether scaling up or down, the IT team always keeps its eye on the cost as well as the quality of service it provides the business.

"We have been searching for a panacea that would allow us to increase, or decrease, users as the business dictates and Star has helped us get there," Quinn adds.

"Despite the fact we are now more virtualised than ever before, the performance of our servers is far superior and the costs are far lower with Star."

The journey continues and Quinn will continue to look at Star to help bolster other areas of the business. Given the valuable lessons it has learnt, Richmond Events is looking for more success and a very innovative, but very uneventful, bright IT future. ■

Sunderland City Council

Forget any notion that all councils are conservative when it comes to IT, Sunderland is set to be a pace-setter for some time

Company profile

Sunderland boasts a world-class university and a rich feast of cultural, sporting and heritage attractions for locals and visitors alike. Having recently gained the accolade of being a Digital Challenge Winner, and with many innovative initiatives in the pipeline, it's also fast gaining a reputation as a highly intelligent tech city. Nissan's base there is the most productive car plant in Europe. The current population sits at around 280,000 people.

HERE'S A QUESTION for a local council leader: what do you do when your city sheds a quarter of its jobs in just 14 years?

Sunderland City Council responded to this challenge with a plan to encourage a number of small software companies to take root in Sunderland. It was a move that could have been construed as revolutionary 10 years ago but, in 2012, those shoots are beginning to bear fruit.

Sunderland's Software City is currently home to 42 start-ups, which are envisaged as being in the vanguard of the move to regenerate the region.

A key part of the transformation taking place is the council's data centre. Built in 2001,it's unusually large for a council of Sunderland's size. With such a facility on its doorstep, the council was in an excellent position to execute on its vision and started casting around for a partner to work with.

But it wasn't a straightforward process.

"The procurement was a very difficult process. We wanted a strategic partnership as there were several risks involved and we wanted a supplier who appreciated that," Tom Baker, head of ICT at Sunderland City Council, explains.

There was a certainly a lot of interest in Sunderland' plans from some leading vendors and the choice was a tough one.

As Baker explains, because the council was treading a new path in the UK, there was little know-how to draw on. "We had some excellent proposals but IBM was the one that stood out. The main problem for us that what we wanted to do was difficult to reference as no local authority had gone down the route we were going," he says.

Having plumped for IBM, the rollout of the new services began. Key to the whole transformation was the move to virtualised desktops for internal council staff and its external partners.

But first came the assessment of current resources. "As part of the process, we started looking at what was being used – that was real eye-opener," Baker says.

"If we had an executive who wanted a laptop and we could see that it hadn't been out of the docking station for nine months, we could instantly save costs by giving him a Wyse terminal."

"If we had an executive who wanted a laptop and we could see that it hadn't been out of the docking station for nine months, we could instantly save costs by giving him a Wyse terminal."

The range of applications being used throughout the council was also cast under the spotlight.

"We saw a massive spike of Microsoft Office – which you'd expect – and lots of apps like SAP and Microsoft Dynamics – which you'd also expect. But there was a long tail of other applications," Baker says.

"It allowed us to sit down with businesses and work out what apps were needed and decommission others."

The council will soon be at the next stage of its plans for applications and will be in a position to offer a basic service catalogue – the council's own version of the government's CloudStore.

"What's crucial for us is that there's a degree of automation and self-provisioning," Baker adds.

The rollout of the cloud-based services has taken longer than expected – something that Baker attributes to the sheer scale of the processes involved. But the council is already well advanced towards where it wants to be.

"It's not just a question of cloud services. We could offer platform as a service or even infrastructure as a service," Baker adds.

Baker stressed this was not about the council going its own way. "This is very much a partnership approach. Training is a big part of the deal - my techies are delighted: they've never had so much training," he says.

While the driver for such a comprehensive overhaul of the council's infrastructure was not driven by financial considerations, the transformation is not without such benefits.

The council can expect to make cost savings of about £1.4 million a year over the next five years, according to Baker.

There could be other financial benefits too. The council is having on-going discussions about the commercial considerations of the services that it's offering.

While the final decision on that is very much up in the air there are aspirations to work with other councils in the north-east and with local fire services, police and health services. Sunderland also hopes to be a partner for BT and the public sector network (PSN) too.

What's most impressive about the Sunderland project is the way that all the parts come together. It's not always the case that the management team and techies are on the same wavelength but Sunderland offers proof as to what can happen when they are. ■

Decisions, decisions: Choosing the right cloud provider

The cloud service provider industry is booming with a vendor to suit every need and budget. But how do you know which partner to trust with your business and its data?

AS WITH TRADITIONAL technology efforts, choosing the right partner to work with – and trust your applications or infrastructure too – is critical.

There are many factors at play in the decision making process.

Contracts are a key concern and an area many get caught out with confusing jargon or seemingly unfair clauses.

Research by the Cloud Legal Project at the Centre for Commercial Law Studies at Queen Mary College in East London suggested cloud providers should be more flexible when it comes to terms and conditions.

"The findings suggest that more customer-friendly terms are being demanded by large cloud users such as governments and financial institutions, and being offered or agreed by niche specialist providers and market entrants - making contract terms a source of competitive advantage," says CLP research consultant, Kuan Hon.

An increasing number of firms are putting the environment front of mind when it comes to selecting a partner.

Sustainability concerns were high on the agenda in recent research sponsored by Rackspace. So much so, in fact, that, for 74 per cent of respondents, sustainability gives a service provider an edge over A N Other provider without such credentials, regardless of whether the two choices are otherwise equal.

US vs Rest of world

The study found disparities between international companies and US-based ones when focusing on green issues. Faced with the choice between two unequal providers, international companies would choose the sustainable option in 60

"We see sustainability expanding from a nice to have to a need to have."

Top 10 tips for choosing a cloud management system

What should would-be cloud businesses consider when choosing the right tool and provider to help build and manage their cloud?

1 **Fundamentals** – Choose a provider with real understanding and experience of what businesses need to successfully deploy a public or private cloud;
2 **True cloud, not just virtualisation** – Insist on functionality that provides maximum automation and efficiency. Above all, find a product that gives you flexibility to adapt to the market as it evolves;
3 **Time to 'cloud-readiness'** – Slow cloud transition risks the need for fresh capital expenditure on new hardware and operational inefficiency of the existing infrastructure. Measure your deployment in days, not months;
4 **Cost** – The cloud management software market is competitive and best-in-class functionality can be yours for little or no up-front investment. There needs to be a very good reason to insist on software with monolithic licensing and prices for integration, implementation and support;
5 **Billing** – Don't assume moving to the cloud means you have to adopt new billing platforms, utility billing models and a small set of billing options. Billing flexibility is critical to your cloud project's success;
6 **Hardware compatibility** – Focus on platforms that support the widest range of hardware types and performance levels, enable you to re-use your existing servers and SANs, and providers that can help with any hardware investments needed;
7 **IOPS monitoring** – Unless you have good reason, avoid cloud management systems which cannot monitor IOPS or that don't offer flexible tiered storage and swap disks;
8 **User permissions** – Look for cloud software that gives you granular control of user limits and permissions, with an API that lets you exploit that control to create exactly the cloud service required;
9 **Usability** – Favour cloud platforms which enable you to customise the user experience easily – either directly or through the API;
10 **Support** – Any IT system will fail at some point. When that happens, you'll need rapid, high quality support. If things do go wrong, you will need SLAs with response times measured in minutes, not hours.

SOURCE: DITLEV BREDHAL, CEO, ONAPP

per cent more cases than US-based ones.

When it comes to influencing purchasing decisions, 72 per cent of US respondents said sustainability is more important when selecting a service provider than cost, compared with 80 per cent of respondents from elsewhere.

Internationally, the majority (91 per cent) build sustainability into their purchasing decisions on either a periodic or standard basis – this figure stands at just under three-quarters for those based in the US.

Countries outside the US seemed to put greater emphasis on weighting sustainability as part of overall buying decisions, according to the Rackspace research.

"We see sustainability expanding from a 'nice to have' to a 'need to have,' as companies understand that selecting solid partners as part of their supply chain translates into lower risk, more efficiency and more reward," said Melissa Gray, Rackspace's director of sustainability. ▶

BIG OR SMALL: Which cloud provider is right for you?

When choosing a cloud provider is big always better? There are many factors in play when it comes to the right choice

WHEN ONE CONSIDERS a cloud service, two providers spring immediately to mind: Microsoft (with Azure) and Amazon (with EC2).

Along with these two behemoths, however, come tens of thousands of smaller companies offering services with the "cloud" label.

"I am not a number," proclaimed The Prisoner's number six, "I am a free man". With these smaller services, there's every chance that you'll be seen more as a customer than as just another amorphous entity (although we're not suggesting the opposite is the case with the larger players either). But is this small fish/big pond situation really all it's cracked up to be?

Is it a white label?

The first thing you must do is find out who actually runs the service. In many sectors of the IT industry a service provided by company A is actually a re-badged service from company B, perhaps with a layer - often a very thin one - of added value dropped on as some kind of motivation for you to sign up with it.

Naturally, added value generally goes hand-in-hand with added cost, so ask yourself whether it's worth it. For instance: If the supplier claims that it has a better relationship with its upstream provider, dig about and find whether the difference is really that significant.

Even if the provider is, say, 10 times larger than you, it may still be a minnow in the eyes of the underlying service provider. Is the added-value service they're offering something you could get elsewhere, even from the upstream provider to some extent, or perhaps something you could do yourself? Is the added value actually just familiarity or locality?

> **"It's perhaps no surprise that there's actually no right answer."**

That is, are you dealing with the white-label supplier just because you know them, and forgetting to do a proper evaluation?

Where's the support?

We've heard tell of a company being offered a service (albeit a more general network service, not a cloud-specific instance) with 24x7 support in the event of a system-down problem. The technical staff of the supplier totalled two, and there was no third party fall-back in place. Unsurprisingly, the company in question declined this offer. Large suppliers have big support teams, and smaller suppliers have smaller ones – QED.

Do not, however, take this to mean that small suppliers can't support you properly. A well-focused, well-trained team looking after a modest portfolio of well-understood products can be far more efficient than a behemoth with umpteen-squillion clients and a vast product portfolio.

In a small organisation, you need to be confident that they have reasonable staff retention (hands-on experience trumps a wad of documentation every time, and you don't get it in a support team with high staff churn) and technical competence. If you can be happy that this is the case, you've ticked the box.

Some of us are actually far more critical and inquisitive when dealing with large companies, because a big team is often a bad thing – particularly when your ticket gets picked up by one of the less capable people on the team. If you go with a big provider you should always ensure there's a comprehensive, properly implemented escalation path and that you know all about it. Better still, ensure you have a named account manager whom you can chase when the effluent hits the fan.

How performant is it?

Big cloud implementations must be resilient and powerful. It's as simple as that. With such competition for business between the big names, performance is king and if one of the providers were to have a significant performance or resilience issue their market share would drop like a stone in no time at all. Let's face it, moving to another provider isn't a big deal if you're not doing anything requiring any major platform-specific features.

You can generally work on the premise, then, that the big players will perform and tick the relevant boxes.

With a smaller provider, you have to be a little more careful. Be absolutely specific about the requirements you have, and ask all the right questions regarding dedicated vs. shared CPU/RAM/disk capacity and the like – ▶

otherwise you could find yourself in a nasty mess later when the provider's client base has grown more quickly than it's been able to grow its infrastructure.

By all means ask it about its infrastructure, drilling right down to make and model level: for instance, it's one thing to know that all its blade servers are connected through 10Gbit/s Ethernet, but quite another to be aware that the 16-port 10Gbit/s blades in the chassis switches are four-to-one contended and thus when flat out on all ports can only give you a quarter of what is claimed.

Is it scalable?

Scalability is a crucial point. Think of your requirements now, then consider an optimistic growth pattern. Then treble it. Then add a bit. Now see how the provider's infrastructure will cope – bearing in mind that you should be considering the same prediction for its other clients.

The huge players are adding kit at a mind-numbing rate in order to keep up with demand; will the smaller providers be able to do so?

Physical equipment and hosting space cost money, but more importantly they have an overhead when it comes to installation and management. The latter should be modest (with automated installation technologies such as Microsoft's SCCM you can run up and test a cabinet full of servers in a couple of hours) but this assumes they actually use a sensible technological mechanism rather than just having a couple of blokes with CDs clicking "Next".

What's the geography?

Cloud customers care about geography. The big players have clear geographies,

with multiple data centres in each region and wads of bandwidth between them. Smaller players may well be limited to particular locations, and the links between them may be puny or even almost non-existent.

Be careful to understand the geography and how it fits your business purposes, particularly if moving from in-house to cloud will cause your data to cross a provincial or national border since you could be piling legal queries on top of the obvious access speed ones.

What's the SLA?

The final, but by no means less important, consideration is the service level agreement your provider is willing to conform to.

There's a simple methodology for evaluating an SLA:

1 Get a yellow highlighter and mark the target uptime figure. Workout the number of minutes per week/month/year the service is likely to be down, and multiply by two;

2 Get a red pen and cross out the bit that explains service credits;
3 Still holding your red pen, cross out any bits that have a guaranteed time to repair;
4 Now ask yourself if your adjusted downtime figure from the first step is acceptable. If not, don't sign up;
5 If the downtime figure is OK, ask the provider to agree that if it gets it spectacularly wrong three times in six months, you can terminate with 30 days' notice. If it says "no", don't use it.

What we've just written probably sounds overly cynical, but actually it isn't. To take the steps in order:

1 What you care about is the downtime. Nothing else. So know what it's likely to be, and be conservative;
2 Service credits are a waste of time. When your CEO is bawling you out because his finance system is down for a week over year-end, he won't give a stuff that you're getting two months' free service;
3 Guaranteed time-to-repair figures are rubbish. Nobody can guarantee such a thing;
4 Think of the CEO and his year-end finance system outage. That is, when considering acceptable downtime, think of the worst possible case;
5 If you're getting dire service, you need to be able to get out.

Interestingly, the components of this SLA methodology fit different size providers differently. The uptime figures are far easier for a large provider to conform with, because, in many cases, they triple up on servers (one live, one hot standby, one staging for migrating to new software versions) and have highly available resources in all other components of the system. But on the contractual side you have a much better chance of getting a smaller provider to agree to your dire-performance termination clauses.

Oh, and stick to your guns. Don't be afraid to drop a $2 billion supplier from an RFP process if the SLA is a key evaluation criterion and it insists that its standard SLA can't be flexed. You may find, interestingly, even though the other two $2 billion-plus providers say the same thing initially that, they do, in fact agree to be flexible.

Weighing up the options

It's perhaps no surprise that there's actually no right answer. But in general, you're going to get a more robust but less personal service from the larger providers.

On the other hand, you'll have a far more flexible service from the smaller guys. But you must be absolutely clear on your requirements and the levels of service you consider acceptable and, more importantly, you're likely to receive. ■

Cloud computing: Who's who?

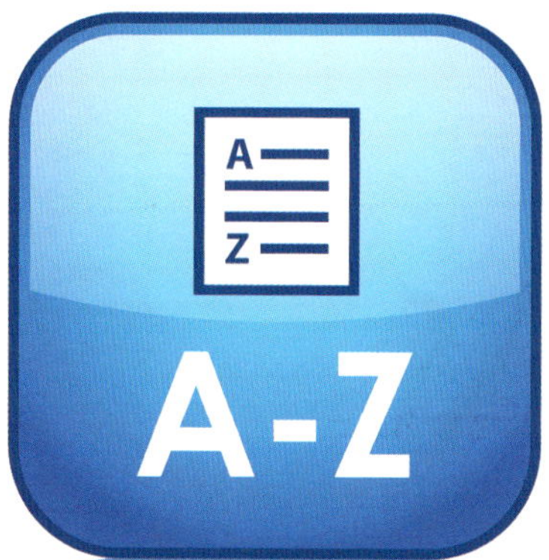

We list the top cloud computing movers and shakers in the industry today. Read on for our handy A to Z

IT'S IMPOSSIBLE TO LIST all the many companies active in cloud computing – so here's a list that includes most of the big players plus a selection of smaller firms. Cloud providers come in all shapes and sizes, but key categories are:

- Infrastructure players, which provide the data centres and management tools to host public, private and hybrid clouds;
- Platform players, which allow many different application vendors to supply a service;
- Application software firms, which have cloud-based systems such as sales, accounts and so on;
- Operation management providers, which offer services such as remote storage.

Some companies are active in several categories and the lines are blurred in any case – this is one of the fastest ever moving sectors in IT.

Akamai

Akamai is a Hawaiian word meaning intelligent or wise. The company provides a distributed computing platform that mirrors content from customer servers on its global platform of servers. Web Application Accelerator is Akamai's IaaS offering, which is designed to speed up the performance of web applications without the client requiring additional infrastructure.

Amazon Web Services

Amazon Web Services (AWS) was established in 2006 and yes, it's part of the multi-billion dollar online bookseller. In fact, AWS uses Amazon.com's global computing infrastructure – which is the backbone of the company's retail business and transactional enterprise – to provide scalable and secure cloud

computing infrastructure to clients. Amazon is one of the giants in the cloud computing space and its offerings are billed on usage.

- EC2 is an IaaS offering that stands for Elastic Compute Cloud. It operates on a simple web service interface, which allows clients to obtain and configure capacity readily, and provides developers with tools to build resilient applications;
- S3, or Simple Storage Service, is Amazon's storage offering, and provides a simple web services interface that can be used to store and retrieve any amount of data at any time, from anywhere on the web, using the cloud;
- Elastic Beanstalk is Amazon's deployment and management service. It allows users to quickly deploy and manage applications in Amazon's cloud. Users upload applications and Elastic Beanstalk automatically handles capacity provisioning, load balancing, auto-scaling and application health monitoring;
- AWS CloudFormation gives developers and systems administrators an easy way to create a collection of related Amazon cloud resources and provision them in an orderly and predictable fashion.

Apple

Apple has enjoyed extraordinary success in recent years with the iPhone, iPad and the Mac computer range, and now adds its iCloud cloud offering to the mix. The service is aimed at consumers who want to store music, photos, applications, documents and so on.

Telcos like BT are natural cloud players

BeyondTrust

BeyondTrust is an American company specialising in privilege authorisation management, access control and security solutions for virtualisation and cloud computing environments. The company's offerings are designed to strengthen security, drive compliance and eliminate the risk of intentional, accidental and indirect misuse of privileges on desktops and servers.

BT

BT, the major British telecoms company of course, now provides cloud computing services including products such as Salesforce.com and NetSuite. BT's Virtual Data Centre offers a range of cloud capabilities, including both public and private cloud systems.

CA Technologies

CA Technologies is an IT management and software solutions company operating across all IT environments from mainframe to the cloud, including both public and private cloud computing solutions. In 2010, CA Technologies acquired Nimsoft, a provider of IT performance and availability monitoring solutions that can be used in cloud applications.

Canonical

Canonical is a UK software firm that offers cloud computing services through its Ubuntu software, which allows users to create a private cloud within their own IT infrastructure or to deploy a cloud with one of Canonical's partners, including Amazon, Microsoft and RedHat. It is ▶

flexible and features frequently updated security procedures.

Cisco

Cisco is a multinational systems company providing communications and networking technology. It's cloud offerings include:

- Secure MultiTenancy – owned collectively by Cisco, VMware and NetApp, this cloud-hosting infrastructure-as-a-service offering uses pre-tested and validated computer 'stacks' and fault-tolerant architecture;
- WebEx – Cisco's collaborative suite that combines real-time desktop sharing and phone conferencing, and allows the sharing of documents, presentations and applications across PCs, Macs and mobile devices. Up to six webcams can be streamed at once.

Citrix

Citrix provides cloud services such as server and desktop virtualisation, software-as-a-service, conferencing, open source products and networking. The company has data centres around the world including the UK, India and Australia. It acquired XenSource in October 2007 and cloud.com in 2011. Citrix OpenCloud is the main cloud computing platform.

CloudShare

Previously known as IT Structures, CloudShare is a California-based cloud provider founded in Israel. It offers a self-service platform that enables organisations to create virtual data centres for a range of business functions including application development and testing, demonstrations, proofs of concept and IT training and certification. CloudShare Enterprise is the main IaaS offering, and other products include CloudShare Pro, a free, individual version of the platform that enables individuals and small teams to manage complex virtual IT environments in the cloud.

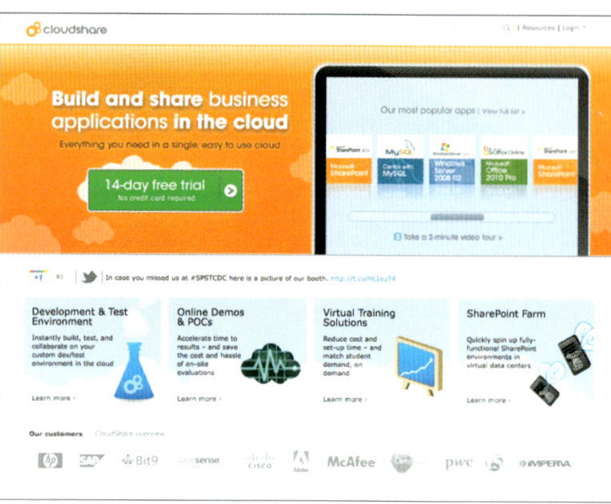

CloudShare enables you to create virtual data centres using a self-service platform

Commensus

A UK provider of a cloud platform known as C-VIP, which operates across five data centres, three in London, and one each in Paris and Frankfurt. It backs its service with a 99.999% uptime service-level agreement.

Dell

Dell is known mainly as a PC maker, but it also provides cloud computing, consulting and data storage services. Offerings include infrastructure management, virtual integration and mobile management services.

ElasticHosts

ElasticHosts is a London-based cloud provider. The company stands out mainly because it charges by the resources required, such as memory, disk, processor and network, as separate entities, allowing customers to create

virtual machines with any configurations they choose. Its scalable infrastructure-as-a-service offerings can run on any OS.

EMC

EMC is a long-standing data management giant that delivers cloud services such as Atmos, a large-scale storage system.

Fasthosts

Fasthosts is a leading UK web hosting and cloud solutions provider. As well as offering a comprehensive range of web hosting, email and server products, Fasthosts is at the forefront of developing innovative cloud solutions for the SME market including virtual servers, SaaS, secure online storage and back-up. Fasthosts developed its own virtual server platform, called DataCenter on Demand, as the foundation of its virtual solutions. In recent years, the company has won the Microsoft Hyper-V Cloud Partner Award and Microsoft's Hosting Partner of the Year Award.

Fujitsu

Fujitsu is a major provider of IT systems, services and products in the UK. Its IaaS offering uses secure data centres with the resilience and performance levels required for business systems hosting. Fujitsu's PaaS offering enables software vendors to reach markets on a pay-per-use basis.

GoGrid

GoGrid is a California-based cloud infrastructure service provider that first began offering cloud solutions in 2008. The company offer cloud solutions hosted by Linux and Windows virtual machines. GoGrid Cloud Storage is a file-level back-up service for Windows and Linux servers.

Google

California-based multinational Google is best-known for its search engine but also provides cloud computing solutions and other internet-based services and products. It was founded in 1998 and runs more than a million servers in its data centres. It operates the well-known Gmail email service, web browser Google Chrome, the Google Talk messaging application and even produces operating systems for mobile telephones.

- Google Apps is the company's SaaS offering, providing customisable versions of Google's own products, including Gmail, Docs, Talk, Google Groups, Sites and Google Calendar;
- Google Cloud Storage enables developers to store and access data in the company's data centre infrastructure. All data is replicated to multiple US-based data centres, has individual and group-based access controls and key-based authentication.

HP

HP, a tech giant producing servers, laptops, mobile phones, printers and scanners, has entered the cloud market.

- Enterprise Cloud Services-Compute offers computational services using HP's data centres. The service is a pre-built, off-premise cloud designed to run core applications with scalability;

Google: a firm that's organised to work in a cloud

- CloudService Automation is HP's SaaS offering, providing a package of cloud-building hardware, software and services.

IBM

IBM has joined other well-known IT brands in offering cloud services, such as LotusLive, a cloud-based enterprise networking and collaboration tool integrating email, social networking for business, file sharing, instant messaging and data visualisation, integrated with Skype, LinkedIn and Salesforce.com.

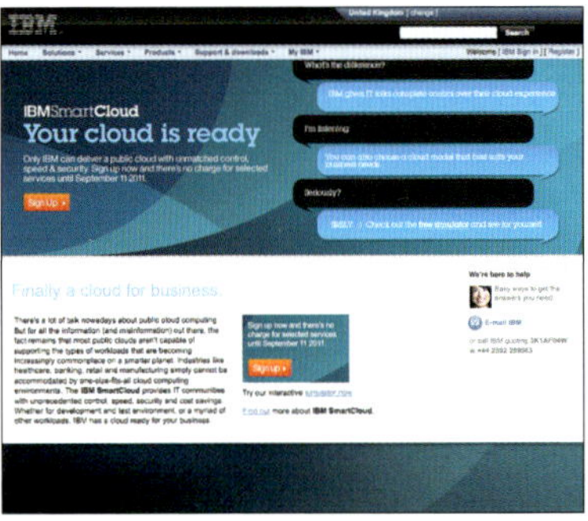

Computing giant IBM recently launched LotusLive

Intuit

The company produces financial and taxation software to service the small business and the accountancy industry. Its flagship products are Quicken, QuickBooks and TurboTax. Intuit now offers cloud-based versions of its applications.

Iomart

UK firm Iomart has figured highly in global rankings of cloud providers. It offers managed hosting and private/hybrid cloud computing based on its data centre estate in the UK, and runs data centres in London, Maidenhead, Glasgow, Nottingham and Leicester.

Joyent

Founded in 2004 and headquartered in San Francisco, Joyent is a software, virtualisation and IT services company specialising in the cloud. It offers cloud services for large online clients, including social networking site LinkedIn (it was also the original host of Twitter). The company is also active in the online gaming industry.

Microsoft

Microsoft has dominated many aspects of computing and has now entered the cloud with Microsoft Cloud Power. In addition to System Center 2012, it has a number of software and platform offerings that use familiar Microsoft interfaces:

- Office 365 is an evolution of Microsoft Online Services and combines Microsoft Office with the advantages of the cloud. Users can access email, documents, contacts and calendars from anywhere with an internet connection;
- Windows Azure is both a software and platform service provided on a pay-for-use model. It offers multiple application development tools, automated service management and a global data centre presence;

Microsoft's Office apps are now making a cloud move

- Microsoft's Business Productivity Suite delivers the company's familiar suite of services from the cloud, including 25 gigabytes of mailbox storage, and access through a variety of mobile devices to key services such as email, calendar and shared content;
- SharePoint is Microsoft's collaboration platform, bringing together familiar Microsoft interfaces and using the cloud to provide a single, integrated location where employees can work with their team members, share knowledge and find organisational resources and information.

NetSuite

NetSuite is a provider of cloud computing business management software. Key offerings include:

- NetSuite's business software incorporates everything from accounting and financial resource planning (ERP) to customer relationship management (CRM);
- NetSuite OneWorld, a cloud-based on-demand system to deliver real-time global business management and financial consolidation to mid-sized companies with multinational and multi-subsidiary operations;
- SuiteAnalytics, which provides real-time business intelligence using real-time dashboards. It uses the cloud to give real-time views of company performance, finance, sales, marketing and service fulfilment.

Nimbus

Nimbus offers business process management software to help its clients capture, manage and deploy their operational processes and supporting information to their workforce, wherever they are, using the cloud. The company is a Microsoft Gold Certified Partner and a partner with SAP, Oracle and Salesforce.com.

Novell

Novell is a US multinational software and services company that offers platform cloud services, including Cloud Manager, which automates complex provisioning workflows, from requests and approvals to creating and employing new business services, and Cloud Security Service, which improves security if a company uses more than one cloud application, through a secure, single password log-in.

Oracle

Software giant Oracle delivers both private and public cloud computing solutions. Clients pay for what they use and have a choice of deployment models using Oracle's scalable cloud infrastructure. Offerings include:

- Oracle Exalogic Elastic Cloud – a platform for enterprise-wide data centre consolidation on any scale, from small departmental applications to large and demanding mainframe applications;
- Oracle On Demand – a flexible deployment model for applications.

OVH

The second largest hosting provider in Europe, OVH provides a number of offerings for customers, whether they're looking for a professional relationship or assistance with a one-off project. It boasts five data centres housing more than 100,000 machines.

Parallels

Parallels provides virtualisation and automation software across all of the main operating systems. The company is working with a group of independent software vendors and service providers ▶

to expand their cloud products for customers of all sizes, including helping large companies to develop in-house clouds.

Plan B

Plan B is a specialist IT disaster recovery business based in the UK. It says it provides 'near instant recovery' of working systems on its Rescue Cloud of remote virtual servers.

Rackspace

Rackspace has been hosting website, applications, email servers, security and storage since 2001. It makes a big deal of what it calls the "fanatical support" it offers to customers and has several levels of hosting services in both the public and private clouds. Offerings include:

- Cloud Files, which provides unlimited online storage with easy upload and speedy file transfer;
- Cloud Servers, which allow you to choose your own operating system, choose a server size and only pay for what you use;
- Cloud Sites, which spreads your traffic across a cluster of servers;
- Jungle Disk and Cloud Drive, which allow small business and personal users to securely store, back-up and share files in the cloud at low cost.

Red Hat

Red Hat is an open source and cloud provider which recognises that each client's IT infrastructure is likely to comprise hardware and software from a variety of vendors. Its philosophy is that you should be allowed to use and manage those assets as one cloud rather than being locked into one vendor and it delivers a number of cloud solutions including its Enterprise Virtualisation platform for businesses with heavy cloud demands.

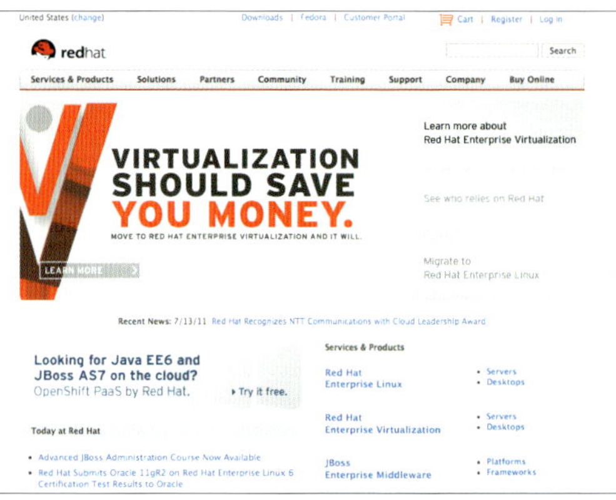

Red Hat's Enterprise Virtualisation platform is ideal for heavy demand

RightScale

RightScale is a cloud computing management company that offers an automated platform for on-demand cloud services. Products include the Cloud Management Platform for reducing administration and the complexity of managing cloud deployments, while still giving flexibility, control and portability.

Salesforce.com

Salesforce.com started as a CRM SaaS provider, and has now expanded into the wider cloud and social enterprise arena. Services include:

- Sales Cloud 2, the main CRM cloud application;
- Service Cloud 2, a customer service platform;
- Chatter, a private social network, like Facebook, which can be used internally in a company;
- Force.com, a cloud platform for business applications, allowing developers to create applications that are hosted on Salesforce.com's infrastructure.

Savvis

Savvis offers a flexible, scalable and easy-to-use cloud interface. It provides public and private network connectivity and has 31 data centres across the world, including in Europe, the US and Asia.

Star

UK-based Star was founded in 1995 and pioneered a cloud-based spam and virus scanning system for business email that eventually evolved into MessageLabs, a messaging and web security specialist. An IT and communications services provider, Star offers email, telephony, hosting and networking, and now delivers a range of cloud computing solutions, including WorkLife, which brings together email, telephony, instant messaging, document management, conferencing and collaboration technology.

SunGard Availability Services

The company provides IT operations support including integrated disaster recovery, managed services, IT consulting and business continuity management software. It offers an enterprise-class private cloud service, a back-up service called Replication-as-a-Service, Electronic Vaulting, for encrypted and secure storage of data that links directly to a recovery system, and a cloud-based continuity management solution.

Unisys

The company has focused on what it considers to be the three challenges that need to be addressed for cloud computing to be viable, namely security, compliance and application rewrites, and migration. It offers solutions across many business areas including finance, budget planning, HR, payroll, email, collaboration, analytics and data storage. Offerings include Virtual Office-as-a-Service, which provides hosted 'desktops' using Unisys's secure cloud infrastructure on a subscription basis. It is designed to simplify desktop maintenance, reduce support costs and improve security compared with traditional desktop PCs.

VMware

VMware offers virtualisation systems and cloud infrastructure from the desktop to the data centre. The company provides private cloud and public/hybrid cloud solutions with safeguards and governance compliance, and clients can build applications that are portable between the clouds within a common management framework.

2e2

2e2 describes itself as an IT "lifecycle services" provider, and the UK firm is active in cloud infrastructure deployment. It says: "We believe that various hybrid strategies – marrying existing dedicated IT investments with either public or private cloud technologies – are the inevitable answer for at least the next five years as the cloud market evolves and stabilises. Cloud should mean reduced costs and rapid deployment of innovative applications, but never at the expense of procurement difficulties or piecemeal, indifferent support levels." ■

Glossary to cloud computing terms

Agility
Can refer to faster, simpler steps for provisioning IT and also wider business processes.

CAPEX
Capital expenditure – the traditional way to purchase IT equipment. Large investments are made in one financial year to benefit the business over the lifetime of the hardware which would typically be three to five years. This is in contrast to OPEX.

Cloud
Simply the global internet, the network beyond your own building.

Cloud backup
Backing up data to internet-based storage systems. As well as being a simple way to backup data it has the added benefit of keeping a copy of data offsite. Disadvantages can potentially include the amount of time to backup and restore files, particularly where data changes frequently and internet bandwidth is limited. Zmanda, Carbonite and Mozy provide services in this area.

Cloud broker
An organisation that acts as a liaison between multiple cloud service providers and customers, by selecting the best provider for particular services.

Cloud bursting
Cloud bursting is a common practice within hybrid clouds to provide additional resources to private clouds as and when they're needed.

Cloud infrastructure
Consists of servers, storage area networks (SANs), networking components and virtualisation software that combine to provide a fault tolerant, flexible and scalable system. Cloud infrastructures are housed in data centres.

Cloud pyramid
A picture of cloud computing layers by functionality, such as infrastructure, platform and application.

Cloud service provider
A company that provides cloud services over the internet. Large data centres are used to run applications and store data in fault tolerant configurations. The long list of providers includes Amazon, Google, Microsoft and Salesforce.com.

Cloud storage
Storage of files on Internet based systems. Cloud storage can be used as part of a SaaS solution where the application and storage are both located on the cloud. Another option is to use it as a store for data that can be transferred

to or from the local network via a web browser or locally installed application. Companies offering cloud storage solutions include Amazon, Rackspace and Microsoft.

Cloud washing
A tactic by vendors, especially software companies, to rebrand their offerings as cloud computing but without true cloud functionality.

Community cloud
A cloud that is shared by a number of organisations with some common interests and aims.

Data centre
Buildings that house cloud infrastructures including servers, storage systems and networking equipment. Also known as cloud centres.

Elasticity
Cloud computing can scale up and down depending on demand.

Hybrid cloud
A system that uses a combination of private and public clouds.

Internal cloud
See Private cloud.

Infrastructure-as-a-service (IaaS)
A service that provides access to virtual servers. In the case of a public cloud, this service would be hosted by a third party and accessed over the internet. It's important to be aware of licensing implications when using this type of service. Services are normally billed on the consumption of resources such as processor and memory. Amazon and Rackspace both offer services in this area.

Mash-up
Combining input from multiple sources in a web application.

Multi-tenancy
A single instance of an application used for many customers, with each customer only able to access their own data. Customers may be able to customise aspects of the software for their data, but only within the limitations imposed by the developers.

OPEX
Operational expenditure costs incurred for services within a financial year. As cloud computing is charged on a subscription basis, it marks a shift from CAPEX to OPEX, making budgeting for IT a simpler process.

Platform-as-a-service (PaaS)
Service that provides a framework for developers to run their own code and so can be used for in-house applications. This service is particularly useful when SaaS solutions don't meet the particular business needs. Publishing applications can be greatly speeded up by using this type of service as the hardware and required components are set up by the provider. Services such as Force.com and Microsoft's Windows Azure fit into this category.

Public cloud
Cloud services provided across the internet by third-party providers. Virtualisation technology is used to provide fault tolerant, flexible and expandable systems that can be divided ▶

up to provide isolated services on a subscription or usage basis. Companies providing services include Amazon, Salesforce.com, Microsoft and Google.

Private cloud
Uses virtualisation technology to provide similar functionality to a public cloud, but is owned and managed by a single user company. Private clouds may be more suitable than a public cloud when highly sensitive information is stored. The large manufacturers such as Cisco, Dell, HP and IBM provide hardware tailored for private clouds.

Storage area network (SAN)
A fault tolerant storage system that can be accessed through fast network technologies to provide storage to multiple servers. SANs work with virtualisation technology, enabling virtual servers to be moved between physical servers on the fly.

Software-as-a-service (SaaS)
A service that provides access to software across the internet, including office applications, email services and customer relationship management (CRM) systems. The hardware and software is managed by the provider, so there is little requirement for local IT staff for this type of service. Providers include Salesforce.com, NetSuite and Google.

Service level agreement (SLA)
Defines the level of service that a supplier will provide, normally including the percentage of uptime and levels of compensation offered if the supplier doesn't meet their stated figures.

Service provider lock-in
The fear that organisations opting for cloud services will be stuck with their original provider and unable to move the data to an alternative provider. Various organisations are looking to create common standards for cloud, the Open Cloud Initiative is probably the best known of these.

Storage service
See Cloud storage.

Utility computing
Providing computing services and charging on a usage basis in much the same way as utility bills. This is a shift from traditional networks where servers need to be purchased and then replaced according to a schedule.

Virtual Private Cloud
Similar to the long-familiar concept of the Virtual Private Network (VPN). Allows organisations to create clouds that look private, from a security point of view.

Virtualisation
Technology used for cloud computing that divides physical servers into multiple smaller virtual servers that each contains their own fully functioning operating system. Virtual servers can be migrated between physical servers and resources, such as processor and memory, and can be increased or decreased as required. VMware, Citrix and Microsoft provide virtualisation solutions. ■